Dr. Joseph Nicolosi

Kent Paris has written
life is not what the Creat
counselees that God mad
erosexual—are leading them onto the wrong path, for there is a way out!
The author's courageous stand has clearly cost him much over the years.
He and his wife have made many sacrifices to pursue a culturally mar-
ginalized ministry. His Spirit-guided wisdom, patience in suffering, personal humility, and caring attitude toward all counselees will be appreci-
ated by the readers of this very helpful book.

Joseph Nicolosi, Ph.D., is author of *A Parent's Guide to Preventing Homosexuality, Reparative Therapy of Male Homosexuality: A New Clinical Approach*,
and *Shame and Attachment Loss: The Practical Work of Reparative Therapy*.

Bob Davies
Director Emeritus
Exodus International

My favorite books are those birthed out of the author's extensive
life experiences, and this title certainly fits that description. For over 35
years, Kent Paris has been on the "front lines" of ministry to persons
impacted by homosexuality, and this primer will be of immense help to
pastors and other church leaders seeking to help men and women with
sexual identity struggles. I highly recommend it!

Bob Davies is co-author of *Coming Out of Homosexuality* and *Someone I
Love is Gay.*

Dr. Don Green
Leadership Studies
Lincoln Seminary

Kent Paris has done it. After more than 30 years of pioneering ministry with those struggling with same-sex issues he has put in print his
profound biblical/theological insights and his seasoned pastoral sensi-
tivity. The same humble servant spirit that he has demonstrated in the
classroom and church presentations for years is evident in this resource
for pastors and care-givers.

This primer is a must-read for every pastor/caregiver who wants to
minister to many hurting families in their flock.

Dr. Charles Self, Ph.D.
Author, minister, professor, speaker

Kent Paris's work is a breakthrough in biblical and psychological understanding. There is no finer manual available to those who are committed to human wholeness. Compassion and conviction, Scriptural depth, and interaction with contemporary literature are integrated into a work that is accessible, cohesive, and comprehensive.

I have known Kent personally and professionally for over 20 years. He navigates skillfully between the Scylla of fundamentalist self-hatred and the Charybdis of liberal narcissism. The moral clarity of Scripture is united with the ambiguities of real case histories to produce a work of pathos and principle.

Human beings are much more than their sexual passions. The radical GLBT movements want it both ways. On the one hand, they claim that the homosexual orientation is predetermined by our DNA. On the other hand, they affirm the fluidity of gender identity. Paris exposes the flaws in their arguments and helps the thoughtful reader see the complexities of the human psyche that is affected by subversive ideological thinking and sin.

If we are going to restore sanity to our understanding of human health and have any future for strong families, we must heed the insights and warnings contained in this prophetic work. Paris is more than a caregiver—he is a herald of hope and holiness in a culture awash with platitudes and relativism. It is refreshing to have Scriptural absolutes shine through the challenges of three decades of life experience.

This will be the manual for all who want to help liberate men and women from the captivity of self-destructive patterns and see every person flourish.

MEANS
of
GRACE

MEANS *of* GRACE

A PRIMER FOR
THE UNDERSTANDING
AND CARE OF SOULS AFFECTED
BY HOMOSEXUALITY

KENT A. PARIS

CP PUBLISHING · JOPLIN, MISSOURI

Copyright © 2010
College Press Publishing Co.
Toll-free order line 800-289-3300
On the web at www.collegepress.com

Cover design by Brett Lyerla

International Standard Book Number 978-0-89900-981-0

Caring for the Flock
Series Introduction

Shepherding evokes idyllic images of green pastures, fluffy sheep, and carefree shepherds lounging in the grass. But shepherding is not all lazy days spent by a babbling brook. Shepherding involves hard work; in fact it can be downright demanding. The sheep, unfortunately, do not possess an enormous amount of intelligence, and they find themselves quite often in need of the shepherd's care and assistance. So the shepherd spends his days watching for predators, caring for injuries, searching for strays, delivering newborn lambs, and directing his flock to the right pastures.

It is in these images that God chose to communicate not only how He cares for us, but also how church leaders are to care for the church. We see in the New Testament admonitions to "be shepherds of God's flock," "be examples to the flock," and "keep watch over yourselves and all the flock." And the very word that Ephesians 4:11 labels "pastor" finds its roots in the Greek word for shepherd. God's people are led by modern-day shepherds, and while you won't see a minister extracting thorns from a member's wool or directing the Sunday school class with a staff and rod, he performs the same types of tasks. Preachers, elders, deacons, and ministry leaders are frequently seen counseling a grieving widow, teaching from God's Word, or celebrating a baptism. It is through the everyday tasks of church life that leaders exercise care for their flocks.

We want to spur your growth as a shepherd. The goal of this series is to encourage spiritual wholeness, the development of leaders, and counseling skills. As you minister to your congregation, you will face situations that stretch and challenge you, so you will find these books a concise and ready reference. It is our desire that the Caring for the Flock Series will help address the needs and concerns every shepherd faces.

This is dedicated to the one I love.

It would be quite easy for me to compose a lengthy acknowledgment of people who have had a significant, positive influence in my life journey and ministry. But, this first book is a milestone, and is the fruit of a truly shared life and labor. Therefore, I have chosen to dedicate this book solely to my wife. She has helped God keep me on my course so that I could help others. Her deep faith and love for Jesus has been a constant source of strength for over three decades of ministry—to me and to our family. She has provided unconditional love, comfort, encouragement, and understanding during trying times. She is the wind beneath my wings, my soul mate, and best friend. Sherri, my love, I dedicate this book to you.

Scope and Purpose

The concept of this short treatise is a brief overview of the nature and impact of homosexuality within the context of the Christian Church, with pastoral guidance and considerations for those who minister in this area.

Foreword

The Means of Grace arrived on my desk in one of those weeks when the entertainment industry seemed to be carrying on one of its aggressive public relations campaigns for homosexual affirmation. The media blitz was in stark contrast to this document from Kent Paris. The "stars" were speaking in simplistic, black-and-white terms while *Means of Grace* is rooted in a factual, holistic awareness of the circumstances related to homosexual practices in our culture.

This book enters a cultural scene where one can realistically identify an ongoing culture war—a battle for the control of institutions, relationships, legal frameworks, and generally accepted values. Those who are promoting revolution are identifying anyone who disagrees with their intended extreme outcome as ignorant, bigoted, and hopelessly tied to the past. Too many Christians, committed to the concept that God has spoken authoritatively through His Word, nonetheless have taken the bait and have engaged the battle on the wrong terms. God still calls His people to act in love—persistent, pervasive, and assertive love. *Grace* enables the activating of such love in a way that facilitates well-informed caring for both victims and victimizers, proffering an enlightened and determined approach that will apply in such public arenas as churches, schools, and community interactions, as well as in the intimacy of families and marriages that are facing the challenges of homosexual impulses, thoughts, actions, addictions, ideologies, and oppressions. All of this is presented in the context of Christ's call to every Christian to be His disciple.

I have observed Mr. Paris's personal, spiritual, pastoral, and professional development for over 35 years as he has consistently engaged the Christian worldview in its encounter with the challenges of contemporary culture. He and his wife have paid a significant price to maintain integrity of ministry, never wavering from a foundational approach of loving the people God loves, caring redemptively for the victims of tragic life choices. Though it is not presented as a testimonial, this work is indeed a testament to God's work in a most reliable, faithful ministry.

Dr. Paul E. Boatman, Dean
Lincoln Christian Seminary

If I profess with the loudest voice and clearest exposition every portion of the Word of God except precisely that little point which the world and the devil are at that moment attacking, I am not confessing Christ, however boldly I may be professing Him. Where the battle rages there the loyalty of the soldier is proved; and to be steady on all the battle front besides, is mere flight and disgrace if he flinches at that point.

Martin Luther

(Luther's Works. Weimar Edition. *Briefwechsel* [Correspondence], vol. 3, pp. 81f.)

The Apostle Paul's Prayers for Believers

Ephesians 1:15-19

For this reason, ever since I heard about your faith in the Lord Jesus and your love for all the saints, I have not stopped giving thanks for you, remembering you in my prayers. I keep asking that the God of our Lord Jesus Christ, the glorious Father, may give you the Spirit of wisdom and revelation, so that you may know him better. I pray also that the eyes of your heart may be enlightened in order that you may know the hope to which he has called you, the riches of his glorious inheritance in the saints, and his incomparably great power for us who believe.

Ephesians 3:14-19

For this reason I kneel before the Father, from whom his whole family in heaven and on earth derives its name. I pray that out of his glorious riches he may strengthen you with power through his Spirit in your inner being, so that Christ may dwell in your hearts through faith. And I pray that you, being rooted and established in love, may have power, together with all the saints, to grasp how wide and long and high and deep is the love of Christ, and to know this love that surpasses knowledge—that you may be filled to the measure of all the fullness of God.

Table of Contents

Preliminary Considerations
Pastor, What's Your Job?

*"The ministry of the cure of souls, or pastoral care consists of helping acts,
done by representative Christian persons, directed toward the healing,
sustaining, guiding, and reconciling of troubled persons
whose troubles arise in the context of ultimate meanings and concerns"*

(Ralph Underwood, *Pastoral Care and the Means of Grace*
[Minneapolis: Fortress Press, 1993] 2.).

If you don't mind, let's begin with prayer. I especially like this
one; it just sets my mind in its proper place with my Maker, before
I undertake a great task.

The Means of Grace, and for the Hope of Glory

The General Thanksgiving

Almighty God, Father of all mercies,
we thine unworthy servants
do give thee most humble and hearty thanks
for all thy goodness and loving-kindness
to us and to all men.
We bless thee for our creation, preservation,
and all the blessings of this life;
but above all for thine inestimable love
in the redemption of the world by our Lord Jesus Christ;
for the means of grace, and for the hope of glory.
And, we beseech thee,

give us that due sense of all thy mercies,
that our hearts may be unfeignedly thankful;
and that we show forth thy praise,
not only with our lips, but in our lives,
by giving up our selves to thy service,
and by walking before thee
in holiness and righteousness all our days;
through Jesus Christ our Lord,
to whom, with thee and the Holy Spirit,
be all honor and glory, world without end. *Amen.*

Book of Common Prayer (1979 ed.) 58.

A world-class theologian did a survey of the church in the west regarding literature produced in the last couple of centuries on the subject of pastoral care. The greatest contributors to Christian essays and works on this subject in the 1800s quoted or cited over two hundred references of early church fathers and the counsel of the church in their guidance to the care of souls. The top ten Christian authors in the 1900s quoted at length from Freud, Jung, and modern psychological models without one reference to church fathers (Thomas Oden, in his work on *The Care of Souls in the Classical Tradition*).

While thankfully there has always been a healthy blending of both the tools of modern psychology and biblical wisdom by dedicated and skilled Christian counselors and caregivers, we have landed in a world where largely the mainline psychological community is not on the side of biblical morality any more. Were it not for dedicated Christian men and women who give themselves to study and practice in a balanced way, there would be no hope for it. More and more we see well-intended but untrained servants of God become more polarized from the advancing social agenda that not only mocks the church, but also is aided and abetted by the manipulation of the social and psychological sciences. Believe me, it takes courage to be a Scott Peck, a James Dobson, or a Joseph Nicolosi. I am sure they pay a price for their voice and their efforts. I thank God for them, and many others, every day.

Nevertheless, when reading from supposedly helpful Christian literature on counseling subjects dealing with homosexuality, we often find that they have become quite polarized in their efforts to deal with this societal problem. Too many who minister will over-simplify and say that this is just a sin problem and the person just needs to get over it. The rest largely engage the client with an approach based entirely on a secular therapeutic model where effort is made to avoid any "sin" or "God" language altogether.

The point of this humble contribution to the pile of Christian essays on this subject is that pastoring often gets lost in the shuffle. Do you want to be helpful to all who come to God for grace? Then in this new century, here in America, you had better prepare to be able to articulate the "Means of Grace" to the person struggling with homosexuality, as well as to the people of God in the parish/congregation where you minister.

This means, if you are the minister/pastor of a flock, then be the pastor. And do not confuse your job or role in this matter. As you read chapter four of this book, you will be hearing a true story, which illustrates well that no "one" Christian helper could ever work through that crisis alone.

If you want to help all who come to God for grace, you should prepare to articulate the "Means of Grace" to the person struggling with homosexuality.

Never forget the basics, the stuff of being human. This book is talking about homosexuality, yes, but underneath that, this book is talking about persons, human beings. Please be reminded that all persons need a human touch to thrive. Infants who are profoundly denied a human nurturing touch in the earliest moments of life fail to thrive. If they survive, they are often marked with serious intellectual deficiencies, not to mention social ones. Humans never lose that need.

Now if someone walks into your office hurting and frightened, bearing great pain at the deepest core of who he or she is as a person, how will you help them? At their very moment of exposure and great humiliation, they often find themselves deprived of their faith community, self-exiled or isolated by the shunning of their own family, and sorely overwhelmed by an avalanche of labels being slung by folks who loved them only yesterday. Now, if you as one who ministers in God's Name, have no tools to de-escalate the crisis, if you have no message of hope, and you thereby deny them the means of grace which can lead to a future free of struggle—a future of peace—then it may have been better if you had never accepted the appointment. And all of this can be avoided if you will remember your role as a counseling minister or pastor in this multifaceted problem.

Pastor, What Is Your Job?

Get this right, for your job is needed, and you are the best and only one who can do your job. What do I mean? Cannot others encourage, counsel, disciple? Surely they can. But they cannot do this with the authority of that one person the client or the client family has chosen as their shepherd. On the other hand there are a tremendous number of unchurched Christians, who will often seek the Christian counselor when they find themselves in crisis, for they do not themselves have a pastor.

In the pages of this primer, I am going to address you as pastors and as ministers of souls. I am not going to acknowledge your denominational or nondenominational status, or what Communion you serve. I am addressing you as men and women of God who have been called to counsel and to minister grace and hope to others as God leads you. I am addressing an audience of people who are already Christian, and beyond that great invitation have been called to service in leadership ministry. I am specifically addressing the ministers and pastors of churches and Christian counselors, where you serve God first, by tending His lambs. It is for you this book is primarily written.

This primer, I believe, will be a rich source of information and insight into the subject of homosexuality for the caregiver, and even for the lay reader just wanting to gain some insight as to the nature of the subject of this book. I believe that God made human beings in such a way that they do need a shepherd. The wisdom literature of the Old Testament puts people in three categories. There are people who have a hireling. There are people who have no shepherd at all. And there are those fortunate enough to have the

Lord, who in both Testaments is the Good Shepherd of His Sheep. He knows them, and He calls them by name.

A friend of mine spent some time in social services as a break from his many years in local church ministry. He told me that he got some new perspectives from the sheep vantage point that he had somehow missed in his work with the church. He relates that when he was first on the job, he took all his ministry skills into the home of a single mother who was in imminent danger of losing her children to the state. She had no help in caring for her four children; she was totally dependent on welfare; she had a drug problem, but there was no one to keep her children if she did go into rehab. And all her friends were in worse shape than she was. She had been depressed, and "smoked" her rent money, and was about to be evicted. When he entered such homes, he found that he was usually met with a whole lot of attitude. He would often go back to the office after a long day of in-home interviews complaining to his supervisor about how uncooperative his client families were. "These people are so resistant," he said, venting to his advisor.

The clinically licensed MSW (Master of Social Work) responded, "They're not resistant, they are reluctant! Do you think you are the first social worker who has ever gone into that home telling them how things will work out and be better? They have no hope; they do not believe it anymore. Why should they believe you? They're afraid to even try to believe again. You're a minister, I thought you would be onto that one."

The next time he was out on a call, he left his notepad in the car, knocked on the door, and sat down with the woman of the house and invited her to tell him "her" story, because he cared about her and her children, and he wasn't leaving until he heard her side of it. He said things worked a little better after that. Pastor, remember this when a family brings in a teenager who is struggling with his or her identity as a "homosexual," that there is a story behind the presenting problem. Your first job is to get them to talk, and your real first job is to listen.

Both Christian and secular therapists have known for several decades that the foundation upon which most mental illness is based, is an erroneous and very subjective view of reality. In his early works, Scott Peck would talk about situations where transference was involved, and about counseling therapy as a "process of map-revising" (*Road Less Traveled*, 46, 49).

People take wrong turns in life and can come up with the most destructive spin and narcissistic motives in which they wrap them. Soon, life is viewed in a completely skewed manner. Their lives become more neurotic and impulsive. Boundaries shift and are justified in the mind of the individual whose internal thought life is in a constant courtroom, judging, rationalizing, in unrelenting tension, and full of conflicting and angry or lustful voices. What therapists often try to do is roll back the clock, take the road map, and see where things got off course. Many Christian therapists are very skilled at that. But what they cannot do entirely is *to call them home*.

They can encourage them home, they can prod them home, but sadly, from a therapeutic position, as one who is alongside the individual, they cannot call them home. If we thought of this in biblical terms, we might say that counselors participate in the work of the Holy Spirit (*paraklete*), while the minister, takes on more the role of the Lord's representative. He stands on the porch of the homestead, looking for the son, calling him to come home. Love is still waiting. Hope and faith still yearn.

Sadly, as you will glean from the pages that follow, not every son comes from a home he wants to return to. This is a great parable when it is God the Father standing on the porch waiting for

> **Sadly, not every son comes from a home he wants to return to.**

junior to come home. But this person's nuclear family, while looking really good from the outside, may have a bit of what we all have: flaws and damage. There are simply fathers and sons who do not get along. There are many men in our land who do not understand what they need to do and be as fathers, dads, even husbands. You will learn about gender voids in this book, and many other factors that promote the development of homosexuality and later manifestation of this lifestyle. But again, it may well be that the teenage son who is in your office, may not want to spend even one more moment back in his father's house. While he may or may not be right on that one, one thing is for sure: that person is in no place at this moment to decide once and for all that he or she is gay.

Near the end of this book you will find more material on clinical assessment, interventions, and resources. Always remember as we minister to those who have lost their way, that people can seem so very assured and determined, while in truth are themselves so very confused. Just that people "think" they need God, or that they "try" to seek Him is of itself insufficient. Counseling and discipleship will be attempted at one of two levels. A man either sees his Christian walk as finding a place for God in his personal story, or that man will seek to find his humble place in God's Story. I cannot overemphasize this point. It is pivotally important. If your stance as a minister is to get people to make room in their life for God, you will fail. You truly need to help them see that it is God who has made room in His life for them; there is no life outside of a God-life. The Apostle Paul writes: *"I have been crucified with Christ; and it is no longer I who live, but Christ lives in me; and the life which I now live in the flesh I live by faith in the Son of God, who loved me and gave Himself up for me"* (Galatians 2:20, NASB). This is just a little more than "somewhat" important as you tackle the deeply entrenched Enemy rooted in the core of the souls of these persons.

All stories, all lives belong to God and are part of God's story. We do not have separate stories—that is the Lie that began in Genesis, that Adam could have his own story, separate from the Father's. Life is a constant flow of choices. There are always spiritual considerations to each and every daily activity. There are always spiritual consequences. True freedom is to live in the joy of your God life. Every man is free to seek and find his place in God's greatest story. And God promises that if they will seek it, they will find it. Not a bad deal!

I hope the insights in this primer will help ministers/pastors and Christian helpers better understand the work that needs to be done. One quickly sees that this must be a team effort, with different people bringing different gifts to the persons in this situation. And we hope that the faith community where you serve has the maturity, the heart, and mercy gifts to love broken people who are often on long journeys home. For in the work that needs to be done, pastor, you are dad. Your church, your people—the Body of Christ—is the home he or she needs to come home to. Working out things from the past with clients and their nuclear families may take years, indeed, it may never happen. But working out things with God and his people, that *must* happen.

You have a very big job, you have an individual struggling with his sexual identity and he (or she) is in crisis. He or she has a nuclear family where there are possibly children and relatives who are confused and maybe quite angry, often not seeing their own part in a complex family system dynamic. They may not participate at all in your counseling interventions. Depending on the circumstances with your church family, there may be some tension to work through there as well. Everyone is going to need his shepherd. This can be a moment when each and every one of them feels threatened. And on top of that, you have a town, a community, a school district, and sometimes courtrooms and prisons in which to stand with them, and by them.

Yours is a work I hope you are called to, for as I am sure you know, especially here, you will need God's help at every turn. *Do Not Forget to Pray for All Your People!* Of all the blessings written in the New Testament, my favorite is the one in St Jude. "Now to him who is able to keep you from falling and to present you without blemish before the presence of his glory with rejoicing, to the only God, our Savior through Jesus Christ our Lord, be glory, majesty, dominion, and authority, before all time and now and for ever. Amen" (vv. 24-25, RSV).

God uses ministers/pastors, teachers, counselors, and encouragers, in His efforts to bless people every day. Let me introduce you to some real situations.

Life Is What Happens
When You Had
Something Else Planned.
Now What?

In this chapter you are going to meet a few people at the very moment of an event that will launch a sustained crisis in their life. As you read through these vignettes of actual life situations, please remember that each and every one came to our counseling ministry by way of a referral from a minister in a local church. These churches were from a variety of denominational and nondenominational/ independent brotherhoods, churches filled with good common folks, not unlike yours or mine. Let me tell you about Susan.

Susan and her husband—both in their forties—were actively involved in their local church. They had three children, ages eight to sixteen. One day, Susan left her workplace earlier than normal, and her entering the home was unnoticed by their oldest son, Daniel, whose bedroom was in the basement. As Susan went downstairs to check on things, she heard curious sounds and laughter. She hesitated at the door and then quietly opened it. Susan was not prepared for what she saw. A teenager she had never seen before was naked, in Daniel's bed, with covers up over his lower half. Their clothing was in piles on the floor. Her son was under the covers, and out of sight. The boy froze as Susan approached them. "Daniel?" Suddenly her son emerged from under the blanket, red-faced, with a frightened expression. Susan managed to stay calm, directed the boys to get dressed, and for the one to go on home. She went to the phone and called her husband. *Family crisis!*

Jim was a highly respected elder in his church, a pillar in the community. He and his wife, Nancy, had been high school sweethearts—a storybook history of the model Christian young couple destined to touch the lives of many by their devotion to Christ. Their daughters were honor students, involved in multiple clubs and devoted to youth activities in church. But Jim held a deep, and long-kept secret. He had struggled with homosexuality since he was twelve. Nancy knew nothing of his struggle, but her world was turned upside-down late one Saturday night. All three of their daughters happened to be spending the evening with friends, and Jim seemed especially on edge. Finally, he turned to Nancy and said, "I have something I must tell you. It has never been my intention to hurt you. I do love you and always have, but I have never been fully honest with you. At first I hoped my love and commitment to you and Christ would be all I needed. I hoped some things from my past would fade away, Nancy. But they have not. I'm gay and have been my whole life. I have tried to change, tried to be what I always wanted to be—normal. But I'm not, and I can't go on this way. I'm so sorry, but I have been seeing a guy for a year now, and I am in love with him." *Crisis!*

Carol and Bill had been married for five years. They had no children. Bill had grown up in a church-going family but his father left much to be desired as a husband and parent. Affection had never been modeled in his family of origin. Bill's father was a hard working, stoic, emotionally detached man. Bill's impression growing up was that women were to be submissive servants in the home, caring for the needs of the husband and children in a most self-sacrificing manner, with little or no expression of thanks. This was a woman's place in the home and a good, godly woman would simply do it. Bill never saw any affection expressed between his father and mother while growing up. Once they were married, Carol quickly discovered that Bill was not a nurturing soul. He was not romantic, neither was he sensitive to or observant of her feelings. When I asked Bill if he could describe what intimacy is, he replied: "That's when you kiss and hug a little and have sex." Bill equated intimacy with having intercourse.

Carol had a growing void within her—a hunger for "true love"—for a gentle, caring touch, for conversation and a soul mate.

She had also begun to form a very close friendship with Beth, a single, younger woman. The two seemed to have so many things in common. No topic was off-limits. Both were strong *"feelers,"* and both felt a unique sisterhood, a safe place to open their hearts and hurts to the other. Slowly, Carol spent more and more time away from home, even into late evenings with her friend. Bill confronted her about his displeasure over this friendship and her lack of affection of late (sex). It was a heated argument that ended in Carol saying she needed space from Bill. That night at Beth's they crossed a boundary, kissed, held each other, and became sexual together. Carol decided that what she had always really needed was the love of a woman. The next day she left a note for Bill expressing her desire for a divorce. Bill called his minister. **Crisis!**

Lisa was a very gifted, highly motivated individual. She possessed unusually perceptive, visionary skills as a business consultant. She had nearly finished her M.B.A. when she married Peter. She was a pronounced extrovert, able to comfortably, confidently move in any social circle. Peter seemed the perfect complement when they met. He was more introverted and inclined toward relationships where he could invest much time and deep conversation. He was sensitive, kind, attentive, and creative. He was a master at interior decoration, aesthetics, and quite the chef. He truly enjoyed pleasing Lisa in all of these areas. She was more pragmatic, cerebral, and oriented to the workplace. Lisa found Peter's orientation toward home to be a positive in their relationship. The match seemed great in many ways—and was—but there were many issues that lay underneath, waiting for attention and resolution. They were not insurmountable, but carried the potential for serious problems. Peter was a struggling graphic artist. Lisa provided the stable income for the two of them. His income was never commensurate with hers. Sometimes it was good, but sometimes he would have literally weeks between jobs. This began to cause tension. Lisa was frequently gone out of state consulting with major firms. She was not supposed to be home until Monday afternoon but her brilliant acumen provided quick, excellent counsel for her client, enabling her to return early. She wanted to surprise her husband. He had seemed particularly down over his lack of work when she departed. It was late, after midnight, and she assumed Peter would be asleep. She quietly entered through the back door, hoping not to disturb him. She started upstairs but heard the television on in the den. The scene she encountered left her shell-shocked. Peter was lying on the floor naked, viewing a homosexual pornographic movie, masturbating. *Crisis!*

Rick is a pastor. He happens to be in a denomination that has itself been struggling with the issues of the gay movement in our society, and how they as a group of churches would posture themselves in the midst of this ongoing culture war. Rick is a family man—wife, three kids, a dog, goldfish, and two hamsters. But Rick is never free of his secret war, never letting on to anyone how he struggles and wrestles with passions and temptations. One night when his wife thought he was on the road and would be getting in late from a speaking engagement in another community, she got a phone call from the county jail. It was Rick and he needed "bailed out" in order to get home. He explained that it was all a terrible mistake, that he was very tired and since he was little more than half way home, decided to pull over in a neighboring community in one of their local parks. That night, the police had done a sting operation to clear the park of excessive gay sexual activities, and he insisted that he was innocently caught up in the sweep. When his wife came to collect him, the sergeant at the desk mentioned that there was another guy in the car with Rick and asked if she was offering bail for both of them, or just her husband. *Crisis!*

Chrissy is seventeen, a junior in her private Christian high school, and a computer whiz. One night when working on a term paper in her bedroom, her computer froze up, and nothing she did seemed to remedy the situation. Frustrated that she would have to start the whole assignment over, even if she could get the computer to reboot, she gave up, and asked her mom if she could use her brother's PC. He had flatly refused her request in the spinoff of recent sibling rivalries. Mom told her to just go in and use her father's computer in his private den—he was out of town that night anyway—but not to disturb anything on his desk. A few minutes later, mom had finished the dishes and went to check on the daughter. She looked into the room and found Chrissy quickly shutting down the computer. When she asked her if she was already done with the assignment, Chrissy dismissed the subject abruptly, said she was going to her room and seemed very angry. Curious, her mother turned on the computer and saw that as the machine loaded, the instant message system had engaged and that one of her husband's good friends had sent some photos of young boys having sex with older men. The messages and the photos were explicit. She ran to her daughter's room and knocked, but Chrissy was crying and refused to open the door. *Crisis*!

These are a few actual stories shared by my clients through the years. In most of these cases, I was the first to provide pastoral intervention and counsel. My first point is that many pastors do not and will not offer counseling in this area of human behavior, frailty, and sin. I am also pointing out a shift that has occurred in recent years in the Christian community. Homosexuality *was* a "topic" that if mentioned at all in a sermon, was simply warned against by preachers to their congregants. Having declared unequivocally that homosexuality was an abomination and that those who do such things will go to hell, they could "feel" themselves off the hook. But in more recent years, most churches of any size have these issues surfacing within their congregational families. Pastor, preacher, minister, youth minister, and teacher, you have members in your church who are dealing with these issues. Now, the people in our churches do not just need to be warned and informed, they need to be gently taught, counseled, led and discipled.

In the past there would be people in our churches who struggled, but who would never approach their own minister. This was a subject that seemed so shameful, so taboo, and so unapproachable, that on most occasions it was only dealt with because of an event that brought matters to the surface in a way that could not be ignored. Things have changed, and now, with growing momentum in recent years, many more people in our churches are approaching ministers with family problems related to homosexuality. While it is a positive change taking place—that people will see themselves more free to seek help—it then calls forth a new challenge for those in ministry. Here again, the church is largely unprepared to counsel, or to minister in this area of sexual brokenness.

The incidences of Christian parents discovering that their son or daughter believes he/she is gay has dramatically increased over the past decade. Homosexuality surfacing as a crisis in married couples within the church has also come to the forefront as a common problem ministers will face in their churches. The discovery of same-gender struggles in the lives of church staff or those serving in some capacity within the church congregation is also now commonplace. The initial pastoral response to such a crisis is monumentally important. But most churches have never developed a biblical paradigm of "normal Christian sexuality," and now find themselves especially ill-equipped to judge rightly this issue in light of the Word of God.

All this is even further complicated by the fact that within the kingdom, there is division among churches, and among groups of people within our parishes who have bought into the secular society's spin on this subject. This issue in the culture at large has radically moved toward a great public acceptance of a very non-Christian lifestyle. (This will be commented upon in a later chapter from the viewpoint of the DSM III, a psychological evaluative reference guide among professionals.) Surely we all have noticed that cultural and social pressure has become so great that whole church denominations have aligned themselves not on the basis of the gospel, but on the basis of their own constituent pressure regarding homosexuality. Unfortunately, to the rest of the kingdom, this is a major shift away from biblical norms, worldview, and authority, and sorely fractures the unity of the holy Christian church at large.

I believe and hope you will discover this book to be a valuable, practical resource guide, helping to inform, to illumine, and to begin in the task of equipping you to effectively accomplish your calling to minister truth and grace to persons who are the focus of God's redemptive love in Christ.

What Is Homosexuality?

What it is; what it isn't. What is the cause; what is the choice?
What is the truth; what is the spin?
What names me as a person?
What is the challenge to the church in this culture war?

A pastor friend of mine has said, "One of the biggest challenges to ministers of the gospel of this age, is not to simply teach
about the Kingdom, but rather it is the great work of un-teaching.
This is always necessary so that people do not misconstrue truth
when they hear it." This is the challenge today more than ever,
especially within the subject matter of this primer! The first purpose
of this chapter is to answer the question, "What is homosexuality?"
The second, to unmask the lie of the politically driven gay agenda
that attacks the Church and society on every front.

In this chapter I have attempted to lay a foundation, step by
step, referencing Holy Scripture, as well as responsible research,
and to add that to what has been commonly known to all people
in all generations. The quote in the opening statement of this chapter is about un-teaching the current spin of the culture so that a
bigger concept of what is true can even get into the minds of men,
especially churchmen. I suppose it is an *apologetic* approach, but
arguably, this is written with a style of phrasing—and perhaps pas-
sion—that the local Christian leader or counselor may need to
adopt in order to effectively communicate good ideas and biblical

principles. This must be done to supplant the false half-truths that lay the groundwork of sexual sin in this focused group of people. Please read this chapter carefully and get the idea of it into your own thinking as a pastoral caregiver.

Defining Homosexuality

One would think that those working within the social sciences would share in common the answer to the question "What is homosexuality," but this is not the case. You would think that the staggering volume of a century worth of published psychiatric literature detailing the common pathologies observed in tens of thousands of people suffering from homosexuality would convince everyone, even the skeptic, that it is a treatable disorder—but that it *is, indeed,* a disorder.

This was the case once upon a time until the 1970s. In a stunning, bloodless coup, gay activists pulled off an amazing overthrow within the APA (American Psychiatric Association) that changed the course of American psychiatry (and ultimately public policy) regarding homosexuality to this day.[1] Here is a little historical perspective. The seizure of power within the APA was a major victory for gay activists—a watershed event, really. Ronald Bayer asserts that the outcome of the vote to remove homosexuality as a mental illness from the Diagnostic Statistical Manual used by professional clinicians, ". . . was not a conclusion based upon an approximation of the scientific truth as dictated by reason, but was instead an action demanded by the ideological temper of the times."[2]

This pressured decision by a sufficient majority within the APA laid the foundation for revolutionary change in American law, in our educational system, and in our churches. Within the field of psychology, the prevailing, medically established view of homosexuality for over eighty years was that homosexuality was a treatable, psychosexual disorder, developing primarily as a result of identifiable environmental and relational influences. Terms like *abnormal,* *deviate,* and *illness* were commonly used to describe same-gender attractions and sexual acts. Because of our cultural context, everyone in Christian ministry should know at least a summary overview of why and how this respected, collectively held perspective within the scientific community suddenly and radically changed. Lacking this overview, you will find yourself at a distinct disadvantage when trying to minister to people struggling with homosexuality, and with their loved ones. Having this overview will especially aid your ability to preach and teach from a balanced, well-informed position. Believe me, some of your clients will appeal to the psych-spin of the day to defend their positions as just another version of normal.

> **Terms like *abnormal*, *deviate*, and *illness* were commonly used in the past to describe same-gender attractions and sexual acts.**

What is homosexuality? Most dictionary definitions would generally agree that the term *homosexual* or *homosexuality* refers to an individual who experiences sexual proclivities toward members of their own gender. That seems simple enough, and yet, so brief a definition belies the challenging complexity of homosexuality as it manifests itself in many different ways in both genders.

Dr. Ruth Tiffany Barnhouse was the first author I read who used the term *homosexualities* in an attempt to acknowledge the wide range of experiences that frequently fall indiscriminately under the same all-inclusive label *homosexuality*. This "framing" of *homosexualities* has been borne out constantly throughout all my years of ministering to persons struggling with same-gender issues. Referring to homosexuality in its plural form is an effort to emphasize the fact that there are varying degrees to which people are affected and troubled in their thought-life and behavior, as well as significant variance in their sense of identity, sexual orientation, and activities. Let me give you an example of what I'm saying.

I have worked mostly with males ranging in age from 15-55 years of age. A large percentage of them are fixated on a limited age range in their attractions. For some that focus is early teens, for others mid-teens, or perhaps even an exact age. This particular group would not be drawn to having sexual interactions with someone their own age, nor with an older man. Why the specific fixation? Frequently, the age of the person(s) they are attracted to can be linked to a molestation experience in their own adolescence, or to their sexual awakening and experimentation with one or more boys their own age. This situation can be compounded if arrested development occurs, sidetracking the maturation process through the teen years. Now we have people "stuck" in their emotional and personality development in the very years that their sense of gender identity and completeness should be in final process. Years may pass, but the primary attraction is fixed.

I must interject that a high percentage of adult male clients confess to feeling like teenage boys emotionally—even men in their 50s have admitted this. They may function well enough in their vocation, but their emotional maturity is strikingly adolescent. This "stuck" phase of adolescence can be much more reality-based than being simply a feeling. The psych groups for many years determined late adolescence transitions into early adulthood for males in this culture around age 25. Too many young men, already in self-denial about their same-gender attractions have chosen to take a wife, thinking that this will either "save them" or "mask them." As you can imagine, this kind of disparity in the emotional development of a married couple can utterly sabotage the wife's expectation of intimate oneness in marriage. It is my belief that the male with same-gender attraction and locked-adolescence issues has no expectation whatsoever for marital oneness. He will deceive his wife because he is deceiving himself. I hear this common complaint from wives who have been thrust into marital crisis due to the discovery of their husband's behaviors.

He will deceive his wife because he is deceiving himself.

The wives frequently confide that they feel like their husbands are boys in many ways, not men. They are terribly frustrated and often angry that their "marital" dynamic feels more like a mother-son than that of a husband-wife. They long for mature, masculine love to be returned to them, for a soul mate, but they gradually awaken to the fact that they are legally married to a "teenager." More than likely this kind of a close, intimate sexual union between a husband and a wife was never modeled out by the man's parents during his childhood a generation back.

I have also worked with males and females whose attractions were toward members of their own gender old enough to be their father or mother. Why not someone their own specific age? What are they looking for? Then there is a large group whose homosexual attractions are mainly focused on persons that are their own age. The point—people attracted to their own gender may vary greatly in who and what they find appealing: specific ages, physical attributes, or personality traits. I will offer a constructive, helpful paradigm for understanding the nature of same-gender attraction shortly, but first let's reflect upon homosexuality from a psychosocial perspective, and later from a theological one.

It's not *politically correct*, but the Christian community must not *shrink* from viewing homosexuality as an abnormal adaptation in human development, and homosexual behavior as aberrant. Over sixty years ago, a clinician writing for the *Yale Journal of Biology and Medicine* proposed the following definition of *normality*:

> **The Christian community must not shrink from viewing homosexuality as an abnormal adaptation in human development.**

"*that which functions according to its design.*"[3] That is succinct! But for many in a postmodern culture, *design* arguments are irrelevant due to changing views of human sexuality, identity, and relationships. These socially disorienting shifts are the result of the culture moving away from a Judeo-Christian view of anthropology concerning the origin, nature, and destiny of mankind.

That is part of the evolution/*revolution* taking place all around us. Pro-gay activists have worked tirelessly, with striking stealth and success, to inject their radical agenda into mainstream America. When will the Church wake up? Here is a case in point. In the 2008 national election, a group known as the *Cabinet*, comprised of wealthy gays, strategically poured tens of millions of dollars into key campaigns in order to defeat candidates who they determined were *anti-gay*, people who would likely block their agenda. This consortium was affectionately called the *Gay Mafia*.[4]

One of the goals of the gay agenda has been to desensitize our culture to the gay life with the help of Hollywood, television, and the Media (e.g., Dr. Phil, Oprah, Ellen, Rosie, and others, wittingly or unwittingly), brainwashing the public into believing that homosexuality is as normal as heterosexuality. Certainly this is part of the battle over legalizing same-sex marriage. Politically correct thinking regarding homosexuality is prevailing. Once upon a time we were introduced to *tolerance*. Now it appears that anything short of full acceptance and hearty support of those living a gay life is quickly singled out as homophobic, unenlightened, prejudiced, and even hateful. I've been called these labels and far worse. These derogatory terms are particularly leveled against those of us who embrace a biblically orthodox view of human sexuality, thus seeing homosexual acts as being sinful and condemned by God (along with a list of other sexual sins).

> **Anything short of full acceptance is singled out as homophobic.**

The phone rang one afternoon. It was a distraught youth pastor from an area Christian Church of around four hundred members. "Kent, we've never met though I've heard you speak. I'm in over my head. In the last twelve months I have had nine boys ranging in age from 12 to 19 come to me individually, in private. All have confided that they either think they may be gay, or they have come to the conclusion they are. Most have experimented around with other guys. A couple of the guys have older boyfriends. Kent, what do I do?"

I suggested that he casually pose several questions to his teens next time they gathered, asking for a show of hands. One question was, "How many of you believe that you can be a committed Christian living a gay lifestyle?" The next Monday morning he phoned to report what he had learned. When he posed that question, fully *half* of the youth raised their hands to affirm their belief that you can be a practicing gay Christian. He had to assess the impact that public education, pop culture, the media, and peers were having on his young people before he could prayerfully draw up a plan for focused teaching and private pastoral response for the boys who had come forward.

Dare we ask that if there were nine boys who were struggling within this one conservative Christian church, how many girls were there who also struggle? Were there still others, who had not come forward? There will be, you know. What about the adults? How many people in this church of 400 might be wrestling with these issues? We know 2% were (nine boys).

The fact is that we are seeing large numbers of teenagers in distinctively evangelical, theologically conservative churches fall victim to the intense indoctrination of the gay agenda with growing momentum. Honestly, how could they not be influenced unless we are doing our job, with great intentionality, providing excellent teaching on a regular basis? It is our responsibility to counter the lies our youth are encountering in their worlds. What we teach and model in our Christian relationships really matters. We would hope that anyone within our churches experiencing same-gender issues would feel safe enough to approach their ministers for help and counsel. Remember that for them it may be a very courageous decision to approach you at all.

A shaken Christian mother phoned, desperate for guidance. Her thirteen-year-old daughter had just "come out" to her, declaring herself a lesbian. At age eleven the girl was experiencing attractions toward a girlfriend. She was confused and worried enough to seek out the school counselor. The woman listened, and then suggested to the girl that her attractions were an indication that she may be lesbian—on the girl's first visit, mind you!

The counselor went on to meet with this girl on a weekly basis throughout the next two school years, never contacting her parents to make them aware. The school guidance counselor had played a major role in channeling this woman's young Christian daughter toward solidifying a lesbian self-identity. The girl rejected the Christian faith as well. There is a real battle for the hearts and minds of our young people. We must rise up to meet this challenge. We must acknowledge the powers we are up against and take them seriously. We are losing large numbers of our youth to the world, and unless we respond with a proactive strategy to address this culture with a biblically grounded view of human sexuality, we will lose a generation. Our youth are being duped into believing homosexuality is inborn and that people cannot change their sexual orientation. In short, they are coming to believe that some people are gay and some are not, that either way is *natural* because it is "who you are," and that "God made you that way."

We are losing large numbers of our youth to the world.

Is Homosexuality Normal?

Let's explore for a moment this nonsense about homosexuality being *normal*. The American public and much of the Church need a good dose of the facts. Well-established research findings have long revealed the appalling promiscuity and aberrant sexual practices among adult male homosexuals. For the sake of space, I'll take a closer look at male homosexuals as opposed to lesbians. But trust me, there are sufficient, sobering statistics revealing risk factors of sexual behaviors for females as well.

This is the kind of information that is not being publicized precisely because it challenges the liberal assertion that homosexuality is equally normal and natural, simply a different sexual orientation. It reveals the sinful, dark, deviant, desperately driven nature of the gay life. What I'm about to share is shocking and distasteful but important. We are constantly exposed to carefully scripted gay characters on television who appear so normal and well adjusted, so in love with a committed partner—like Ellen portrays. These masterfully scripted theatrical performances have been an effective part of the ongoing effort to normalize the homosexual lifestyle in America and to brainwash the public—especially our youth—that the gay life is perfectly healthy and normal. One claim of the gay community is that gay relationships aren't any different than heterosexual ones. I beg to disagree.

In the early 1990s, the University of Minnesota Hospital and Clinics published a major study entitled: *Demography of Sexual Orientation in Adolescents.* The study drove home what we all know: the reality that adolescents are still in a very formative stage of development throughout their teen years. The finding undergirds our legitimate concern for their vulnerability to outside influence. At age twelve, for example, 25.9% of the children interviewed in that study were "unsure" of their sexual orientation.[5] This has far-reaching implications. Those boys and girls who experience common developmental worry over their sexual orientation—like the twelve year old girl in our story—are far more vulnerable to sexual experimentation or pro-gay indoctrination if there is a void of solid, respectable teaching and information being shared with them from their Christian sources. It is a well-estab-lished fact that adolescents are far more prone to making impulsive choices based on emotions and hormones rather than out of a carefully laid moral base. So what happens when you discard the moral base completely?

What happens when you discard the moral base completely?

The troubling challenge we face today is a public educational system so infiltrated and influenced by pro-gay propaganda, that an even higher percentage of kids are exposed to educators, school counselors, and student support groups who are complicit with the gay agenda. They aid in erroneously labeling many of these kids as homosexual or lesbian at a totally inappropriate stage of life development. "Counseling of a sexually questioning teen need not encourage premature self-labeling. Initially, it is sufficient to acknowledge the student's experience of same-sex attraction; later, how to proceed in counseling should be determined by the student and his parents . . ."[6] It is not just wrong ethically; it is evil! For an eye-opening booklet on this topic, see *Teaching Captivity: How the Pro-Gay Agenda Is Affecting Our Schools . . . And How You Can Make a Difference* (Love Won Out Series).

The following statistics are not pleasant things to contemplate, but this is the dark side of the gay life that you don't often hear about, if at all. This is not the *gay* life that is so idealized and dressed up for media consumption (scripted propaganda), not the tidy *gay* life our youth are intentionally being taught about in school. This is the true reality behind the stage props, behind the funny *Will and Grace* impressions. As you review these studies, you will see that the behaviors surveyed demonstrate that the gay community has largely eroticized these debased practices in place of true human sexual intimacy. You cannot be intimate with a thousand people, most of whom you never met before. Sadly, too many are so given over to this erotic bondage that they later find themselves at a place of no moral conscience at all.

Studies indicate that the average male homosexual has "hundreds" of sex partners in his lifetime. In their study of the sexual profiles of 2,583 older homosexuals published in the *Journal of Sex Research*, Paul Van de Ven et al. found that only 2.7% claimed to have had sex with one partner only. It found that "the modal range for number of sexual partners ever [of male homosexuals] was 101-500."[7] A further 10.2 to 15.7% self-disclosed having had between 501-1000 different sexual partners over their lifetime. An additional 10-15% stated they had engaged in sexual relations with more than 1,000 sexual partners.

In his study of male homosexuality in *Western Sexuality: Practice and Precept in Past and Present Times,* M. Pollak found that "few homosexual relationships last longer than two years, with many men reporting hundreds of lifetime partners."[8] The notion that homosexual relationships are no different than heterosexual relationships is a baseless, misguided fallacy. Remember, our discussion is revolving around the notion of homosexuality being *normal*. Consider the following statistics from one research study:

❖ 98 % report anal sexual relations

❖ 92 % report oral/anal sexual activity

❖ 78 % report participating in group sex

❖ 73 % of adult male homosexuals have had sex with boys, age 19 or younger

❖ 42 % report "fisting" where the hand or arm is inserted into the rectum of their partner

❖ 37 % report sadomasochism

❖ 32 % report bondage

❖ 29 % report urinating on or in their partners

❖ 17 % report eating and/or rubbing themselves with the feces of their partners

❖ 15 % report sex with animals

❖ 12 % report giving or receiving of enemas for sexual pleasure[9]

Normal? Healthy? I think not. One of America's best-known monthly gay magazines is *The Advocate*. In a survey published in the magazine in 1994 revealing the sexual preferences and behaviors of 2,500 homosexual men, a select portion of the findings included:

Sex acts homosexual men say they love:
- ❖ Insertive oral intercourse 72%
- ❖ Receptive oral intercourse 71%
- ❖ Insertive anal intercourse 46%
- ❖ Receptive anal intercourse 43%
- ❖ Receptive anilingus (tongue in the anus) 45%
- ❖ Insertive anilingus 29%

Sex acts they engaged in (last five years):
- ❖ Three-way sex 48%
- ❖ Group sex (four or more) 24%
- ❖ Bondage & discipline sex 20%
- ❖ Use of nipple clamps 19%
- ❖ Sadomasochism 10%

Where they met their "partners" (last five years):
- ❖ Bar/disco 65%
- ❖ Bathhouse, sex club 29%
- ❖ Adult bookstore 27%
- ❖ Park, bathroom 26%
- ❖ Roadside rest area 15%[10]

Because the average reader may be uninformed as to who is doing these studies, let me point out that it is not mainly conservative political action committees funding this research, but it is the data put out by the gay community themselves. Astounding as that may seem, as you can clearly see by the last cited source above, it is their own publication who is reporting this. One might think, how bold, how in your face. Truly, these statistics indicate anything but *normal*. To the person with any sensibilities this appears almost nonhuman. Keep in mind as you begin to see the magnitude of these concerns—what the additional implications are for those who actively engage in homosexual acts with multiple partners. Beyond the sexually transmitted diseases, there is the bodily physical damage, other disease pathologies, mental illness, alcoholism/chemical dependency, and suicide.

Risk Factors

Let's just look at the risk factors for people engaging in gay sex to contract a wide range of sexually transmitted diseases (including HIV). This survey further revealed:

❖ 26% of HIV-positive men who have had insertive oral intercourse have had sex most typically with someone they have just met.

❖ Among men who have had insertive anal intercourse in the past year, 44% had sex with a partner without a condom. Among those who had receptive anal intercourse in the past year, 58% had a partner who had sex with them without a condom.

❖ Among HIV-infected men who have had insertive intercourse in the past year, 19% had sex without wearing a condom.

❖ Anilingus (tongue on or in the anus) is fairly common: when asked in the survey about sexual activities in only the past year, it was reported that
   ❖ 41% have performed it, and
   ❖ 47% have received it.

But perhaps one of the most troubling statistics is that among men who had a positive result from an HIV antibody test, only 11% have been honest enough to reveal that they would say, or imply to another that they were "HIV-negative" [not infected with the HIV virus] in order to have sex with that person.[11]

As a Christian counselor, I wish that I could say that only unbelieving, godless pagans engage in these many behaviors listed in the various studies, but sadly that is simply not true. Easily 98% of all of the clients I have worked with over three decades either loosely wore the name *Christian,* or seriously considered themselves to be Christian brothers and sisters, just like you and me. Though my clients come from widely varying faith backgrounds and churches within a 300-mile radius of Champaign-Urbana,

Illinois, clearly most of them come from strong evangelical and conservative churches like yours and mine.

And, of course, they sit next to us on Sunday mornings. They are often well-respected, married, and serving in a leadership capacity within your church. That brother, this sister may be a close friend or beloved member of your congregation. But we must keep in proper balance here that homosexuality is not the only manifestation of sexual sin and brokenness among our own church members, our friends and associates. Even so, before they came to me, they were first in your churches, in your faith communities, and this remains so. A typical pro-gay view would insist that being homosexual is their normal, natural condition, or true self. There is now a fairly impressive though utterly errant gay theology that is convincing a multitude of gullible people that there is no "contradiction" between being a Christian and a practicing homosexual, lesbian or a transgendered person.

Self-Identification

One of the fundamental errors people experiencing homosexuality make is the decision to embrace a sexualized identity. "I am gay," "this is who I am." This self-perception is certainly understandable given their life experience. One must exercise compassion here, but the fact remains that this is a false identity from both a psychological and theological perspective. Our sexuality (and sexual behavior) is a dimension of our humanity, but it does not comprise the sum total of a person as a human being. Man is immeasurably more complex and expansive in his divine creation than what he might find to be erotic, and to whom he finds himself sexually attracted. Dr. Lawrence Hatterer, author and psychotherapist, who spent a great deal of his life dedicated to assisting homosexual "strugglers," has written, "The homosexual does not exist—only persons who fantasize, feel, and act homosexually exist."[12]

> Our sexuality is a dimension of our humanity but not the sum total of a person as a human being.

I use his reframe as a therapeutic tool. When I say that self-labeling is powerful, I mean that both positively and negatively. Working as a Christian counselor, I am helping to move a human soul from one who has about zero self-esteem into one who sees himself as a child of God who can again love himself and accept God's grace. Reframes are powerful; Jesus truly moves us out of a story of fallen darkness in Adam, and into His own Body as Christians and children of light. Paul says that once a slave to sin; he is now a slave to God. What potent images of change and redemption.

Now this "frame" can also be problematic. All Christians know that we must get "real" with God as we turn from our sins and follow Jesus. And we do not want to communicate that a person who has stolen was not therefore a thief. But at the same time, I object to those in the Kingdom who suggest to others that these negative labels are now their "lifetime" labels. They are not. That is not the big picture in Christ. But it is part of the Deceiver's plan.

During the long and hard work with clients trying to find their way back, one of my favorite frames concerns the "Lie" of the Deceiver juxtaposed against the "Truth" of God's Son. The Deceiver has told the client that he is a _____ (fill in the blank). But that is a lie. God tells us that He has made us all, and that indeed, we all belong to Him. We in Christ are doubly His, and we all need to walk in this call regardless of our temptations, and in spite of our frequent missteps. So when Dr. Lawrence Hatterer offers the reframe as he did in the quotation above, I believe he is right on target. We are working toward the goal of a shift in self-perception, helping establish the individual in their true identity in Christ.

Biological Influence

Another avenue used by Gay activists seeking to normalize homosexuality within our society is an appeal to human genetics. They have intentionally used distorted or falsified information in order to mislead the public into believing homosexuality is genetic in origin. Furthermore, they have sought to discredit any and all research that would suggest otherwise.[13] They actively pursue the censure of contrary information. But, the groundbreaking, convincing genetic research they hope for has not surfaced to date.

This has not stopped the gay movement from citing numerous "research findings" purported to the public as newfound validation supporting the theory that people are born gay, only to later have these projects discredited. Such false reports are then never corrected in the public's view. Honest, good science and God are not at odds here. Genetic theory itself holds court on the notion that homosexuality is genetically driven. The overriding results of all genetic research and theory is that biology at the human DNA level, with all that it does, is driven to be capable of reproduction. If biogenetics fails in this, then nothing in the biosphere would be stable. Humanity would probably not even be here to discuss it, as every eruption of life would be a one-time anomaly. Hence, in the history of biological studies, science describes genes within organisms as *maladaptive* if they lead or direct the organism to a place where it cannot reproduce itself. To spell this out succinctly, gays argue that they are driven to homosexual relationships genetically, while all that they do in their homosexually driven behaviors would clearly fail in reproduction.

Please understand that energetic research is being done by groups on both sides of these issues. For example, some recent biological research suggests less of a genetic influence than a hormonal one where there is interference with the prenatal masculinization of the developing human brain (see NARTH website). Still, "born that way" or "influenced that way" does not indicate normality.

This is not that complex, but somehow this corrective has been overlooked by many, and intentionally ignored by a gay-friendly media. This argument from the gay left is wanting the public to buy the idea that homosexuality is genetically passed on from generation to generation while at the same time "underplaying" that no homosexual, gay or lesbian, can reproduce themselves without the assistance of an opposite gender mate (donor sperm, donor egg, artificial insemination procedure and/or donor womb). So therefore they know that their "gene," maladaptive or not, is present in a way that it would die out in a generation unless the subsequent generation also "mates" with the opposite sex through human engineering. Thus, again, in a Darwinian sense same-gender attraction would be maladaptive and undesirable.

If the reader could indulge my sarcasm here, let me say that we understand that you can take an occurring gene and make it to be maladaptive. Through selective breeding and science you could produce something that you would later enter into a dog show as a little ball of fur that used to be a dog, or the state fair as a new hybrid tomato. Does the gay movement want Americans to view them as genetically engineered hybrids? Do they wish humanity to be a race of fertile hermaphrodites? What you have on the political Left is a great push to make science sound like it supports the homosexual agenda, when much more plausible explanations are at hand. So much of the rest of human behavior is learned, and therefore we simply make choices to fulfill our passions and lusts. But with overwhelming media and entertainment/Hollywood support, this gay spin on human genetics, becomes more a propaganda machine than a scientific tool or argument. Maybe everybody should take a deep breath and just reread B.F. Skinner, the famous behavioral psychologist, and turn off the news and the Hollywood sitcoms.

We have a higher authority with a clearer message on the subject of homosexuality. There will be more reflection upon homosexuality from a biblical/theological paradigm later in this chapter. I will also comment further on the power of labels.

Clearly, the greatest source of information where one can find such an impressive library of solid scientific research, articles, and resources in support of reparative therapy of homosexuality is the organization called NARTH (detailed information in the annotated bibliography). These professional men and women work tirelessly upholding the legal right of persons to seek such therapy. They are countering the falsehoods propagated by gay activists and the liberal media and providing credible research to support the reality that people can change. You must appreciate how important the genetic argument is to the gay agenda. They have fought to make this myth our prevailing cultural understanding. What is the motivation? It is to escape responsibility and to sidestep moral implications. You see, if homosexuality is a fixed part of me as surely as my blue eyes, then I have no *personal responsibility* or

The motivation is to escape responsibility and to sidestep moral implications.

choice in the matter. And so we hear, "How dare you judge me and tell me I need to change!"

This is the very reason why gay activists and the gay community are fighting so fiercely against those of us in the Christian communities who are providing spiritual and psychological assistance in helping those who view their homosexuality as being in conflict with their faith, beliefs, and life goals. Most notable among the chief players on the front lines of this culture war are Exodus International, NARTH, and Focus on the Family. Through various forms of Christian counseling, participation in support groups, or through a more traditional, psychoanalytic approach like *reparative therapy*, tens of thousands of men and women have found effective help in learning how to "manage, control and overcome" homosexuality.[14] This turn of phrase is one I first heard from Dr. William Consiglio, author of *Homosexual No More*. These brave people have experienced and documented genuine change in their lives. While much of the world is skeptical, such transforming inner growth should not surprise Christians (1 Cor 6:9ff; 2 Cor 5:17ff).

We asked the questions at the beginning: What is homosexuality; what causes it? Generally, most credible, respected scientists share the perspective that the development of homosexuality is complex—a mysterious interplay between "social, psychological and biological factors."[15] But saying there may be biological factors at work in the development of homosexuality is not at all the same as saying people are born gay. Most within the scientific community would agree that the environmental factor plays a central role in the gradual development of same-gender confusion/deficit. In my seminars, I have stated that there are large numbers of psychiatrists and psychologists who still believe that homosexuality is a treatable disorder. Not all have succumbed to political pressure out of fear for their practice and livelihood. But I must also tell you that there are highly respected colleagues in my field who chide me for being overly optimistic.

Environmental Influences

On a weekly basis I am told things like: "I experienced same-gender longings since kindergarten. I found certain boys attractive.

I envied their looks, their athletic abilities, and admired their physique in comparison to mine." What do these attractions or longings indicate? What do they reflect?

The early attractions are not usually erotic in nature unless they were accompanied by sexual violation. Later with the emergence of puberty, the attractions become eroticized and thus further confused. People don't ask for or choose to experience these attractions; they are just there. Please hear that. This is so important to grasp in formulating your pastoral response. Most young people growing up are clueless to the nature of these attractions or the reason they are experiencing them. Then, at some point as they are growing up, individuals make more conscious choices about how they are going to respond to these attractions and longings. Along the way they will choose what significance and meaning they are going to attribute to them. Most young people making these decisions do so largely from a feeling-based self-perception, where their decisions seem to them to be instinctual, but are in reality, need-driven responses. One might also state they are deficit driven. What are they missing? What are they searching for? What are they attempting to fill inside? What are they perhaps trying to heal—albeit in a dysfunctional, distorted manner?

In all of the literature I have read over the decades, no one has captured the developmental dynamic so frequently at work in same-gender attraction better than Dr. Joseph Nicolosi. As mentioned above, he describes SGA as a *reparative effort* or *reparative urge* in his published literature. In an article entitled *The Meaning of Same-Sex Attraction,* Dr. Nicolosi explains, "During twenty years of clinical work with ego-dystonic homosexually oriented men, I have come to see homosexual enactment as a form of 'reparation.' The concept of reparative drive has been well established within the psychoanalytic literature; in our application, the person is attempting to 'repair' unmet same-sex affective needs (attention, affection and approval) as well as gender-identification deficits (Nicolosi, 1991, 1993) through homoerotic behavior."[16]

The Effects of Labeling

Long ago, by conscious choice, I elected to use the term *homosexual* very sparingly. I prefer to speak of persons struggling with homosexuality, or persons who experience same-gender attractions and thoughts. Why? Well, certainly one reason is that labels imposed upon us by others have the terrible power to cause great harm, even to the destruction of our sense of self-worth. Labels carry the terrible potential to impact our self-concept, our sense of identity, and can set into motion self-fulfilling prophecies. Erik H. Erikson, the noted developmental psychologist points this out in his book *Identity: Youth and Crisis*: "If such 'negative identities' [e.g., homosexual] are accepted as a youth's 'natural' and final identity by teachers, judges, and psychiatrists, he not infrequently invests his pride as well as his need for total orientation in becoming exactly what the careless community expects him to become."[17] Labels carry with them the awesome potential for locking the individual into the prison of false identity.

Dr. Barnhouse echoes this warning in particular when dealing with adolescents experiencing homosexual attractions. She notes: "I use the word homosexuality to refer to an adult

> **We must "distinguish the homosexual act from homosexual identification."**

adaptation characterized by preferential sexual behavior between members of the same sex. The emphasis on adult is extremely important. Much of today's rhetoric does not allow for the fact that adolescence is often accompanied by a period of transitional anxiety or confusion about sexual identity. That observation long antedates any discoveries by modern depth psychologies. To lump discussion of homosexual phenomena in teenagers together with those occurring in adults is such an inappropriate confusion of disparate categories as to render meaningful discourse virtually impossible. . . . It is also important to distinguish the homosexual act from homosexual identification."[18]

Barnhouse is stressing the issue of predominance (degree) and persistence (duration beyond adolescence) of a same-sex desire, psychic response, or orientation. These are important distinctions to make when thinking about homosexuality, especially in light of the vulnerabilities of young adolescents who are uncertain about their sexual orientation. Young people are impressionable, susceptible to faulty information and guidance, gullible and open to exploitation from pro-"gay" counselors.

It is understandable that the notion of inborn homosexuality is an oft-made conclusion. It certainly seems to explain the life experience of most persons with persisting same-gender attraction during their developmental years. Most of my client base claim their same-sex orientation has been part of them as far back as they can remember, usually hearkening back to their grade school years. A lesser number identify the onset of puberty as the beginning of their SGA. But normally, this prepubescent, same-gender attraction was not erotic in nature.

Developmental Issues

In an attempt to help this group sort out the past, I have often posed a series of clarifying questions to men who have linked the beginning of their homosexuality to the era between preschool and the onset of puberty. These questions help clarify the true nature of these attractions. Here are some questions meant to assist the client in differentiation. "Do you mean you desired genital sex with other boys or young men when you were four or five years old?" "Did you engage in oral or anal sex at that age?" "Did you even know what sex was at the time?"

Normally the reply is a perplexed *"No,"* to all such questioning. Usually, I'll ask something like, "What do you mean then when you say you were homosexual at age four (five, six, seven, eight)?" They reply, "Well, I was attracted to other boys (young men, or adult males—whatever age their individual attractions were). "I wanted to be close to them physically." Some have responded, "I had very strong feelings for them (ones they reflect upon now as romantic) and wanted to be with them all the time." "I've always had a feeling of being different from other boys . . . of not feeling I measured-up to my peers, of feeling inadequate." "I wanted to see them naked" (a common curiosity). "When other boys were playing games, I stood off watching like a kid looking inside a candy store from the street, with no money. I didn't have the male currency to spend inside. I wished I was like them, but I wasn't at all. It was very painful and the source of constant anxiety and fear."

What are we to make of this? Do these feelings and thoughts plainly indicate latent homosexuality? Can this attraction clearly be interpreted as homoeroticism? Does it suggest an emotional or psychic disturbance? Or could it be a sign or symptom pointing to an underlying and more fundamental developmental issue? It is my experience that the latter is true in a sizable percentage of cases—that the child is experiencing a manifestation of some kind of an emotional deficit. Needs have not been met by the father, and the child is unconsciously reaching out trying to fill those unmet needs.

Let me illustrate this with case highlights of a young teen I counseled for a number of years. John was fifteen years old when he came to me. He was deeply confused and riddled with deep-seated guilt, initially unable to make eye contact. His parents divorced when he was three. His father, a minister, had committed adultery. He had tendered his resignation and, after the divorce was finalized, disappeared out of John's life to places unknown and never returned. His mother remarried when John was six. Unfortunately, his stepfather was emotionally distant, rigid, and at times, abusive in his punishment. No loving bond developed between them. John did not like or trust him. He thus remained *fatherless* in a very real sense.

Now enters Jeff, who was also thirteen years old, who befriended John. The boys bonded quickly and began spending frequent nights at one another's homes. Within weeks of their meeting, they began sexual experimentation, establishing a fairly regular pattern of mutual masturbation over a period of several months. One night Jeff shared a secret with Jim, making him promise to keep it. They went to a local bus depot. Jeff had discovered a year earlier (at age 12) that older men were really "turned-on" by him and that they enjoyed having sex with Jeff. He was an exceptionally good-looking and well-built boy—a much sought after object of their desire. He was able to gain their attention when he wished, and he discovered he could make money "doing it." That night the boys went in separate directions with two men old enough to be their fathers. John very reluctantly agreed to enter a motel room with the man, who proceeded to undress John, and lead the young boy to the bed. Throughout the disrobing process John said he shook uncontrollably and was extremely apprehensive about what was happening. He felt scared and excited simultaneously. Then he shared a very revealing statement with me: "As soon as he put his arms around me and held me close, the fear vanished. I felt loved and secure in his arms." The man performed oral sex on John, and then coached him to do the same for himself (shrewd, obligatory, compromising manipulation). John disliked having sex with him but the physical closeness seemed to meet some deep longing inside him.

As time passed, this scenario was repeated with numerous men. Something in his initial sexual experience seemed to fill a gaping hole in John; but understandably, it also left him with a growing sense of guilt and shame. He felt loved by and secure with a man his father's age. Curious? Not really. Was John's receptivity to such an experience the natural working-out of an inborn homosexual orientation? Was it some insatiable drive to have sex with men? This is not difficult to pinpoint and understand. Here was a lost, hurting boy who desperately needed love, affection, and affirmation from an adult male. When he began counseling with me at age 15, he had been sexually active for nearly three years. He had graduated to oral and anal sex with Jeff, his close friend, on a fairly regular basis, and with the older men where he offered himself for money (prostitution). Over time, he grew to enjoy the pleasure, the attention, and the material benefits of his sexual activity but was ridden with guilt and shame. He became increasingly confused, not wanting to be a homosexual but fearful he was. Oh, I should mention, John and his family attended a relatively large Christian church in central Illinois, and he was an active member of the junior high and high school youth groups at the same time he was sexually involved with men. John's case history is not unlike countless other stories I've heard from clients.

So in the political spin of the day, do these stories seem to reflect *nature* or *nurture*? What is homosexuality? What causes it?

Homosexuality is admittedly a very complex, multifaceted, psychospiritual problem. Research has long indicated multiple factors (triggers) in the development of homosexuality. But the one central component that appears most often is that of a troubled parent-child relationship during the early developmental stages. A strong, healthy relationship at this stage is critical in assisting the child to successfully grow in a secure and well-adjusted manner. If a child is not secure in the love of their same-gender parent (or both parents), they are more at risk to developing a problem with homosexuality.

I am sure that most parents who do understand that their relationship with their child is strained probably do not see the link to the child's inability to achieve a strong, healthy, same or opposite gender-identification. Complex family interactions plus a convergence of outside influences in each individual's case can make it very challenging to sort out. This is where professional counseling can be of such pivotal help.

Theorists over the decades have differed on clinical pathology in this area. Some attribute more responsibility on the part of the mother, while others point to the father as the primary source of the child's developing disorder. In a significant percentage of my clients, while a particular parent may appear to bear more responsibility in a specific case, normally it becomes apparent that both share culpability for their child's confusion. This is in keeping with the vast amount of research data collected over the past century.

Generally both parents share culpability for their child's confusion.

Here we introduce the notion of an *emotional triangle* or *triangulation*. This relational pattern is common among people who struggle and worth highlighting. Dr. Nicolosi writes: "The 'triangular system' describes the theory that mother, father, and son together bring about homosexual development. It refers to an intensely affectionate, domineering, possessive mother combined with a distant, ineffectual, rejecting father."[19]

Clearly, the same-gender void is the more potent factor. But the combination of an opposite-gender transference or projection must be overwhelmingly confusing for the child. For the purposes of this primer, though, let us continue with same-gender father issues. A father void, including a negative father presence, can cause a child or teenager like John more problems than just a homosexual proclivity. These kids who have experienced rejection, or perceive themselves as rejected by their fathers, are very likely to develop neurotic and compulsive behaviors contributing to an unstable self-identity (e.g., research studies on this subject in prison). We have found that this most basic relationship has far-reaching implications (positive and/or negative) for the development of a healthy and centered masculinity. The father's role in a child's development should not be underestimated. The manner in which a father relates to his son has tremendous power.

With John, his primary vulnerability toward developing same-gender issues lay in his father's abandonment of the family, leaving a single mom to raise the babies. John was raised in a world of females: his mother, maternal grandmother, sister, aunts, and female cousins. He experienced an acute absence of males as role models in his life. At age three, John needed a "daddy," and he did not have one. By his teen years he will need a dad, but will already have been on the wrong roads to find one. We have given good space in this chapter to the concept of a *reparative urge*, but let's take this now to another level.

It has been a common misconception through the years that *same-sex love* is the problematic issue, that same-gender love is deviant and utterly pathological. On the contrary, same-sex love (when it is nonerotic) is part of the answer or remedy for the homosexual struggler. Of course the genital activities (oral and anal sex, etc.) are pathological behaviors with serious health risks. But generally, homosexuality, at its deepest cause is not first and foremost a sexual issue. It is a developmental issue. The focus should therefore be upon the person's unmet developmental needs—and wounds where identified (i.e., childhood or adolescent sexual molestation, childhood trauma, divorce, etc.).

A truly positive factor in the aid of the same-gender healing process is in the establishing of nonerotic, wholesome same-gender relationships, particularly with peers. Hopefully this can be done with older adults as well—people seasoned with wisdom and maturity who can lend support and encouragement. Men need the company and brotherhood of men and, conversely, women need the company and sisterhood of women.

The Theological Perspective

Let us now move to more theological reflections on this subject. Because I do work with Christians from so many different backgrounds, I can witness that many have their own spin on what causes homosexuality. Sometimes I feel like the rabbi in the old story who has two people coming to him disagreeing on the age of a horse. The first man says that the horse is fifteen years old, and the rabbi says, "You're right." The second man says that he knows the horse is seventeen years old, and the rabbi says, "You're right." The first man says, "Rabbi, we can't both be right," to which the rabbi says, "And you're right too." Do I believe, personally, in the demonic? Yes, you're right. Does evil have a reality and express itself in our lives? Yes. I pray the Lord's Prayer just as I hope you do. "Please Lord, deliver me from the evil one." Do I believe that in cases of mental illness, that there is a spiritual aspect? Unequivocally yes! Do I believe that Christians who fall into great sin can open the door again to dark spiritual activity? Yes I do.

However, this book is not a discussion on differences in Christian spirituality. It is a book on homosexual issues that are ravaging through all our churches and stealing our children. And I truly believe that Dr. Nicolosi offers individuals who are in the struggle of their lives, tremendous understanding as to how they first made some very bad choices to solve what were very common and normal human needs that all people have, and to tell them that they were not bad people for having those needs. This does not disagree with the idea that when a door is opened to the darkness, that the darkness then has permission to enter.

Surely, we do no one a favor if we fail to identify something that is truly a sin as a sin in some well-intentioned effort to make everyone more comfortable. Many Christians have serious concerns over the long-term impact of the approach that many innovative churches are taking today. Some churches have so watered down the presentation of the gospel, it does indeed make it inviting to the multitudes in that they believe they have no need to change. That's a great marketing tactic for congregational growth, but I'm not sure what it has to do with growing a Christian.

The central most important shift that must occur is the discovery of their true identity in Christ.

In my view, the central most important shift that must occur within the group of people who are same-gender strugglers, is the discovery of their true identity in Christ. That new identity will come primarily through their exposure to the Word of God, through solid biblical teaching, and through a meditative and prayerful conversation with the Lord.

Apart from the plumbline of the Bible, we have little basis to make a judgment about the morality of homosexuality, or anything else for that matter. Cultural norms and taboos shift. In the eyes of many, we simply have personal opinions based upon "our" *religion*. There is a famine in this generation regarding the Word of God. Christians know that the Scriptures speak with absolute moral authority and have the power to call forth faith that transforms individuals and societies. But it must be proclaimed; it must be heard. We have all listened to many discouraged Christians bemoaning the deterioration of the spiritual and moral fabric of our society. I am terribly concerned myself. But this will always be the challenge of being Christ's disciples in any culture. The Word of God is powerful, active, alive, and can call forth faith. Its proclamation and acceptance bring about transformation to individuals, households, tribes, and cultures. Dennis Prager, a devout, Conservative Jew, believes the Torah (Genesis through Deuteronomy), more than any other book or idea is responsible for civilizing the world. He states: "It is the Hebrew Bible that gave humanity such ideas as a universal, moral, loving God; ethical obligations to this God; the need for history to move forward to moral and spiritual redemption; the belief that history has meaning; and the notion that human freedom and social justice are the divinely desired states for all people. It gave the world the Ten Commandments, ethical monotheism, and the concept of holiness (the goal of raising human beings from the animal-like to the God-like)."[20]

The Holy Scriptures (Old and New Testaments) are not silent regarding God's creative purpose and intention for human sexuality (a relationship between male and female striving for oneness in lifelong covenant), setting forth heterosexual marriage as good and normative. We are not left without guidance. Again, our sexuality has far more depth than simple erotic attraction, far more purpose than achieving a pleasurable orgasm with a physically satisfying sex partner. There is great mystery here. Our gender and the expression of our sexuality is truly sym-

God has not left us without guidance regarding his creative purpose.

bolic of a more profound spiritual calling. William Oddie writes: "Man, collectively and not individually, is in the image of God: *'and God created Man in his own image . . . male and female created he them.'* (Gen 1.27) He created them in His image so that they would be born with an instinct for loving relationship . . . completed only by that which is radically distinct, but also radically of the same nature. It is almost the paradox of the Trinity itself."[21]

We are created for union and communion with another, with one who is like, yet different from our own self. Oddie stresses that "the masculine and the feminine cannot remain authentically so apart from each other."[22] Why? Because we call forth the goodness of one another's gender, assisting in the *becoming* of the other, and in the process, find greater completeness and fulfillment ourselves. I live out my true masculinity in relation to my wife, who embodies the true feminine. The issue

How we understand our maleness and femaleness matters more than we could ever know.

of gender identity is a critical one. How we understand our maleness and femaleness, our masculinity and femininity matters more than we could ever know. Look how far we can fall if we are ignorant of these beautiful truths.

Yes, there is a problem in the gender identity of our culture, and the problem is in masculinity. This deficiency is most profoundly centered in men—although there is a *crisis in masculinity* (a phrase borrowed from Leanne Payne) among our female counterparts as well. The reason is that we live among a people who have lost a sense of God, and with that loss went our sense of masculinity. We cannot know our true identity apart from an intimate knowledge of the person of Christ and the Word of God. There we discover who we truly are. It is not only in men that this crisis of masculinity is felt. Our female counterparts feel this deficit to the extreme, and the very rise and power of the feminist movement testifies to the truthfulness of what I say, for it is not a movement toward femininity within the heart of this cultural phenomenon; rather, it is a very masculine movement among women.

To borrow a perspective from the Bowen Theory on family systems (see annotated bibliography), if men truly lose their sense of masculinity, who is left who will pick it up and live it, attempting to keep masculinity within the family of our culture? Our women, in turn, deny their true gender identity, trying to salvage the very basis and source of strength, peace, stability, and vitality within our culture, namely Fatherhood. Many women whose husbands abandon their role and responsibility as fathers are thrust into a predicament of attempting to be both mother and father, to fill in the gaps left by "dad."

It is not ironic that within such a culture as ours, where one might even question the presence of the Spirit of God among the people at all, that by the close of the last century, movements such as PromiseKeepers would erupt. This was not out of the centralized planning and foresight of an informed and gender-balanced church, but simply out of a movement of the Spirit of God across the land in an attempt to bring healing and restore strength to Christ-possessed men of the Kingdom. This fostered hope that the church would then turn to God and thereby be a light to the darkened culture of our times. These movements called men to love their wives as Christ loved the Church; they called men to be involved with their children, to affirm and bless them in their gender identity, therefore calling forth the highest and best from them.

The church must discover ways to assist young people in healthy human and gender development through teaching and relationships. We need to find ways of naming and celebrating the rites of passage for our youth, affirming their entrance into adulthood, with it's clear goal of growing up into maturity in Christ. James Dobson's book entitled *Bringing Up Boys* and its companion for girls are excellent guides during these developmental stages. Another popular author has written numerous books on recapturing the sense of masculinity that many men have found helpful, especially men who have not had fathers who exhibited wholesome, godly masculinity. That man is John Eldredge, author of *Wild at Heart*. We are losing grip in this culture of a clear sense of what it means to be masculine or feminine, where no one cultural standard or expectation regarding gender roles, relationships or family structures rule the day.

The America I knew as a child is no more.

The America I knew as a child is no more. Back then the majority of children even through high school grew up in traditional family households with a mother and a father, within a culture largely still holding to traditional Judeo-Christian morality, ethical values, and spiritual beliefs in the God of the Bible. In contrast, my sons had few friends whose parents were still together in a first marriage. In fact, interestingly enough, one son had two different friends whose mothers were lesbian, and in their own relationships, raising their sons. There was no father, no surrogate male mentor or role model in these boys' lives. My sons and grandchildren will never know the country my wife and I knew as children.

The cultural revolution of the 1960s set in motion changes that would lay the groundwork for transforming our society away from a Judeo-Christian worldview with its clearly articulated, everlasting morals and ethics. Christianity was the foundation of western civilization and certainly our own country's formation. We are in a battle for the souls of our children and the faithful transmission of the Christian faith to this next generation. Our young people need clear teaching and loving, healthy adult mentors.

God is not silent in His view and judgment of homosexual behavior. It is not feasible to include serious exegetical work related to the relevant texts regarding homosexuality in this primer (Gen 1 & 2; 19:1-26; Lev 18:22; 20:13; Rom 1:18-32; 1 Cor 6:9 and 1 Tim 1:10). Let it simply be stated that a biblically orthodox understanding of these passages unambiguously condemns homosexual genital acts. They are explicitly determined to be deviant and sinful. Homosexuality runs counter to the image of God in Man (male/female). Homosexuality cannot achieve interpersonal completeness (*"The two shall become one flesh,"* Gen 2:24, Mark 10:8). Homosexuality is not at all a union of opposites. The Scriptures reveal that same-gender sexual acts are abnormal. But the most extraordinary witness of Scripture, I believe, and the one we must focus upon is the promise of deliverance, of freedom from homosexual practices (1 Cor 6:9ff). This is not just a "church" doctrine; it is a significant record of the impact Christ had upon persons with deep-seated homosex-

God is not silent in His view and judgment of homosexual behavior.

What we must focus upon is the promise of deliverance.

ual involvement. In Christ, we become new creatures existentially (2 Cor 5:17). The genesis of the reorientation of our sense of identity begins in Christ. This process of sanctification should affect the whole of life, bearing testimony that we belong to Jesus. The Bible provides us with a theological perspective that informs and shapes our understanding—a sieve through which we filter the wealth of knowledge presented by the social sciences, and the world at large.

I remind my clients and audiences that the ancient patriarchs, prophets, Jewish rabbis of both rabbinical schools (Shammai and Hillel), our Lord Jesus, His apostles, and the early church writings of the fathers and bishops of the church, spanning thousands of years of Judeo-Christian tradition are all in agreement. Homosexuality is contrary to God's will; it is sin, and all must repent of such behavior if they are to follow Jesus and find their true identity in Christ. It is the inheritance of the church and the Christian family to hold, to honor, and teach true kingdom life to the next generation.

Normally, I do not pull out the most oft-quoted Bible passages condemning homosexuality when discussing this subject unless a person is unacquainted with the true heart of God concerning homosexual acts. I find that a better platform from which to speak about God in all of this is to begin at the beginning: Genesis. Here we find the narrative record of the Creation of Man—male and female in the Image of God (Genesis chapters 1–3). Our biblical and theological grounds for rejecting homosexuality as a viable lifestyle must be established from the outset of Man's creation, which is recorded in the Genesis record. The Judeo-Christian faith has the high ground on declaring moral truth.

If the authority of the Bible is not recognized, the task of building an argument for an absolute standard of morality becomes impossible. You would be building a constructive argu-

The best platform from which to speak about God's desire is to begin at the beginning: Genesis.

ment on air, not on a foundation. Please remember that the Enemy spent over a century and a half attacking the authority of Scripture in this culture as the groundwork of his attacks upon our peoples in this generation. If, however, the same-gender struggler accepts the authority of the Bible as God's Word you are miles ahead.

The Apostle Paul, writing to the Church in Corinth says, "Do you not know that the wicked will not inherit the kingdom of God? Do not be deceived: Neither the sexually immoral nor idolaters nor adulterers nor male prostitutes nor homosexual offenders nor thieves nor the greedy nor drunkards nor slanderers nor swindlers will inherit the kingdom of God. *And that is what some of you were. But [emphasis mine]*, you were washed, you were sanctified, you were justified in the name of the Lord Jesus Christ and by the Spirit of our God." (1 Cor 6:9ff). That people can change is clearly evidenced in Scripture. This will be powerfully exampled in the next chapter.

Chapter Three References

[1] Ronald Bayer, *Homosexuality and American Psychiatry: The Politics of Diagnosis* (Princeton: Princeton University Press, 1987) 101-154; Dr. Joseph Nicolosi, *Reparative Therapy of Male Homosexuality: A New Clinical Approach* (Northvale, NJ: Jason Aronson, 1991) 7-14.

[2] Bayer, *Homosexuality and American Psychiatry*, 3-4.

[3] C.D. King, "The Meaning of Normal," *Yale Journal of Biology and Medicine* 18 (1945) 493-501.

[4] John Cloud and Beverly Hills, "A Gay Mafia," *TIME* (November 10, 2008) 53-55.

[5] Gary Remafedi, MD, MPH; Michel Resnick, PhD; Robert Blum, MD, PhD, and Linda Harris, "Demography of Sexual Orientation in Adolescents," *Pediatrics* 89 (April 1992).

[6] *"Am I Gay or Am I Straight?" Not a Decision to Be Made by a Teenager.* NARTH Fact Sheet, 1998.

[7] Paul Van de Ven et al., "A Comparative Demographic and Sexual Profile of Older Homosexually Active Men," *Journal of Sex Rsearch* 34 (1997) 354.

[8] M. Pollak, "Male Homosexuality," *Western Sexuality: Practice and Precept in Past and Present Times*, ed. P. Aries and A. Bejin, trans. Anthony Forster (New York: B. Blackwell, 1985) 40-61. See also A.P. Bell and M.S. Weinberg, *Homosexualities: A Study of Diversity among Men and Women* (New York: Simon and Schuster, 1978) 308, 9; see also Bell, Weinberg, and Hammersmith, *Sexual Preference* (Bloomington: Indiana University Press, 1981).

[9] This information was reprinted and published by The Berean League, June 1991, 2875 Snelling Ave, N., St. Paul. MN 55113. It was listed in a report of the American Family Association.

[10] "The 1994 Advocate Survey of Sexuality and Relationships: The Men: The Sexual Relations," *The Advocate* (August 23, 1994) 16-24.

[11] Ibid.

[12] Lawrence J. Hatterer, *Changing Homosexuality in the Male; Treatment for Men Troubled by Homosexuality* (New York: McGraw-Hill, 1970).

[13] Jeffrey Satinover, "The Gay Gene?" *The Journal of Human Sexuality*, 1996 (call 972-713-7130) 8; Mark Yarnhouse, "When Clients Seek Treatment for Same-Sex Attraction: Ethical Issues in the 'Right to Choose' Debate," *Psychotherapy* 35 (Summer 1998) 248-259.

[14] Stanton L. Jones and Mark A. Yarnhouse, *Homosexuality: The Use of Scientific Research in the Church's Moral Debate* (Downers Grove, IL: InterVarsity, 2000); Stanton L. Jones and Mark A. Yarnhouse, *Ex-gays? A Longitudinal Study of Religiously Mediated Change in Sexual Orientation* (Downers Grove, IL: InterVarsity Academic, 2007); Nicolosi, *Reparative Therapy*; Gerard J.M. Van Den Aardweg, *The Battle for Normality: A Guide for Self-Therapy for Homosexuality* (San Francisco: Ignatius Press, 1997).

[15] *The Causes of Male Homosexuality*, Fact Sheet. NARTH, 16633 Ventura Blvd., Suite 1340, Encino, CA 91436-1801.

[16] "The Meaning of Same-Sex Attraction," by Joseph Nicolosi, Ph.D. http://www.narth.com/docs/niconew.html.

[17] Erik H Erikson, *Identity: Youth and Crisis* (New York: W.W. Norton, 1968) 88.

[18] Dr. Ruth Tiffany Barnhouse, *Homosexuality: A Symbolic Confusion* (New York: Seabury Press, 1979) 22.

[19] Nicolosi, *Reparative Therapy*, 78.

[20] Dennis Prager, "Part II: Judaism and Homosexuality; Why Judaism Rejected Homosexuality," *Ultimate Issues* 6 (April–June 1990) 4.

[21] William Oddie, *What Will Happen to God?* (San Francisco: Ignatius Press, 1984) 69.

[22] Ibid.

Crisis Management in Home, Church, and Community

This chapter is going to present an actual case scenario which will highlight the momentum of emotional pain that can ravage a nuclear family because of a hidden lifestyle. The ripple effect can be utterly enormous. Excepting names being changed, there are no embellishments in the telling, it is not a composite of situations, and every person in this report, has lived it, suffered it, persevered in it, and kept faith through it, and with the grace of God, survived it.

If you are a minister, counselor, teacher, or in some way a professional caregiver, please read this chapter critically. As this story unfolds, ask yourself some questions (e.g., how would I approach this one? What is the connective tissue between counseling and discipleship for this family? etc.). Life is not perfect, neither is the care we offer others. I hope the events in the lives of this family can help all to see that life can be messy, full of feelings and judgments, ordeals, and suffering, and so often with way too much laid on the most innocent of people. And yet, people in these situations will all ask God, and will also ask you who shepherd and give counsel, the hard questions, like: "How could he . . . ?" "What was he . . . ?" "What will I say to . . . ?" and ultimately, "WHY?" and "why ME?"

Your work as pastor/minister is not just to the person struggling with homosexuality, your commission from God is to take care of His lambs, *all* His lambs, to pick them up when they are cast down, and to sometimes fleece them without butchering

> **Your commission from God is to take care of all His lambs.**

them. A wise pastor once reminded me that you can fleece a sheep a dozen times, but you can only butcher him once. I will have a few other comments at the end of this chapter.

Kay and Joe are a great couple. At the time of this event, Kay was a young Christian woman in her late twenties. Her love for God and her dedication to the church were the natural outcome of her love for her dad, a minister in a small-town church in the Midwest. She came from a tight-knit but dynamic Christian family, and she was now making a good life with Joe, raising their children with the same love and values. Kay loved being on the worship team at her church. She was living her dream—she was working to have a Christ-filled marriage, she was a mother, she homeschooled her children, and she was using her talents in serving the church. All she hoped for as a girl had come true, her father was the church pastor, the congregation was filled with her grandparents, aunts, uncles, cousins, siblings, nieces, and nephews. The extended family was very prominent in different facets of the church's ministry and leadership.

Joe was a great guy, a very likable, engaging young man. His star was rising in the large corporation where he was employed. His keen business sense propelled him into management, and he excelled as a troubleshooter for his company in crisis situations throughout the country. While Joe and Kay enjoyed a prosperous income, the down side of his job was his frequent absence from his family while on his business trips. With each passing year, his responsibilities required an increasing number of days where he worked one, two, or more hours into the evening before he came home to his family. If the phone rang close to dinnertime, Kay already knew the deal.

Kay loved being a mom. She and her small children were already looking forward to the birth of their next child. She was well into the midst of her pregnancy when the phone rang early one afternoon. "Kay, this is Dr. Stevens. I just received the results of your blood test and would like to discuss it with you and Joe together. Can you two come in after hours at the clinic later today?" She naturally asked if anything was wrong, but her doctor explained that he was late for an appointment and simply did not have the time to open the file. He would see her later.

Kay was not prone to worry but her first impulse was to be concerned that something was wrong with the baby she was carrying. But then again, she thought, maybe it was she. The kids were down for a nap. She picked up the phone.

Joe was at his desk when Kay's call came in. She described the brief phone call from Dr. Stevens. "I need you to come home early." After she hung up, Joe sat in silence, trying to process the thoughts flooding his brain. He too had a sickening intuition—one that filled him with dread and panic. Sometime later, in my office, Joe shared the horrors of those moments driving home. His workplace was an hour drive away. He was numb as he began his trip home. His mind was racing with any and all options open to him. He could simply disappear. He could keep driving and move to California. He could smash his car into a concrete overpass at high speed and end it. Or, he could face it and confess his sin to his wife—no matter what the consequences to follow. Joe had been very successful in hiding his other life; he knew that Kay had no idea. In his gut he feared the worst. But something in Joe caused him to opt for choice three. He choked down his own fears and drove on home to Kay.

"Kay, there are things in my life I have kept from you." His eyes filled up and he choked back the tears as he pulled back the curtain on his secret. He told her the highlights of his poor behavior and passions. Joe's shocking confession left Kay numb. Feeling as though she was trapped in a nightmare, and unable to wake up, she suddenly realized that the Christian man she had been married to for nearly a decade, the father of her children, had become a stranger. His tears, his apology, his plea for forgiveness was becoming a confusing voice in the struggle she was engaging just to understand her new reality, in the wake of this horrible news.

Dr. Stevens delivered the chilling diagnosis that Kay was HIV-positive. Joe confessed to their doctor his secret, homosexual activities. This occurred in the early days of the AIDS epidemic. "This is terribly difficult to discuss, but we must. Joe, you and the other children must be tested." Kay had just quit nursing her youngest child. "Based upon current research, your unborn child has a 20%-50% chance of survival. You need to get your house in order, deciding who will raise your children. Statistically, the odds of either of you living beyond a year are against you. I'm so very sorry." They all sat and cried. Their physician was a fine Christian man. "I will walk with you through this."

Let us break from the story for a moment. Of course I am reflecting on this as a counselor who was called in to help in the midst of this family crisis. But what if you were the pastor of a church where Kay and Joe attended. And remember, their parents, the kids grandparents are members also, and let's say that Kay's dad

What if you were the pastor of a church where Kay and Joe attended?

is the chairman of your church board, or a lead elder in your congregation. Don't forget that there is a matter of other people in that church; some of them are brand new members.

Because you live in a small town, all the children in your congregation go to the same school. It is likely that Kay's kids will not be home-schooled much longer. How are other parents going to feel about the common drinking fountain in the church fellowship hall, or the bathroom? Will they speak their fears, or will they just make an excuse and find another church to attend? In most cases like this one, we are heading to a divorce. There will be some in the family who are mad about that. If Kay and Joe stay together, there will be brothers and sisters of Kay, with kids, who may be mad about that too. And they are not just extended family; they are also your church members.

In a small town, we have not even begun to list the ramifications yet on the daily unfolding of new "Hells" which have to be faced and endured. Then there is Joe's job. Does he still have one? You can always find an excuse to fire someone, and Kay does not work outside the home, nor is she trained to do anything other than what she has done. She does currently run a daycare in her home for a couple of kids to supplement the family income—this will have to stop right away. It may not matter; she may be dead in a year. Who is going to take care of her surviving children, if there are any? Who do you give your kids to? I don't mean to make light of this, but most preachers would rather go through a major building program than touch this one. You must know how preachers hate building programs.

Joe told me once that in those early days, he would go to the local grocery store to pick up bread and milk and cereal. People would back away at the check out lanes, the cashier would often stick to business with her head down, lay his change on the counter without speaking, saying nothing until he had taken his groceries and left. Not everyone would keep silence though, and much of the time it was hurtful. Before you judge that too hard, pastor, remember how it is in a small town, everybody is kind of an extended family, and people can feel betrayed in certain circumstances. Please remember also, that while folks can have a variety of opinions among the townspeople about homosexuality, just about everyone feels the same way about AIDS.

> **Most preachers would rather go through a major building program than touch this one.**

Let's consider the church. Have you ever known people to get upset when someone has harmed their friends? Do people ever take up one another's offenses? How many churches prepare themselves to minister Christ in a pastoral way in such extreme circumstances? How many ministers spend adequate time in sermon preparation to pastorally educate and equip members to keep faith in times like these? In my experience, if ministers/priests deal with this subject at all, it is usually to say simply that the Bible is against it, and then to go home to their Sunday dinners thinking they have done all that is necessary and to enjoy a nap.

Kay's world had been shaken and the safe harbor of her marriage destroyed. Whatever sense of security and comfort still existed lay in her parents. At her insistence, she and Joe asked her parents to come over to the house once the kids were put to bed for the night. Grandpa and Grandma were about to be confronted with the most complex, severe pastoral crisis of their years in Christian ministry. Understandably, their priority and allegiance lay with Kay and the grandchildren, not Joe. He was ordered to move out by the weekend and banished from all church gatherings. After telling her parents the devastating news, the aftershocks jolted the extended family of both Kay and Joe. Soon, the local church they attended would be thrust into a disorienting crisis. And again, in a small town, news spreads fast!

When I began counseling with Joe, the possibility of suicide was very real. He was forced to move out of the family home and in with his mother. He was told not to attend the same church. Arrangements were made for him to begin going to a sister church where he would enter an accountability relationship with the pastor. He was also required to periodically meet with two elders. I was meeting with him twice a week to provide strong support, prayer, and encouragement, frequently several hours at a time. I met with him for around a year and a half helping him to work through many issues that were relevant to the development of homosexuality in his life, including childhood sexual abuse.

At this juncture I also began meeting separately with Kay, and then periodically with the two together. This was an extremely delicate, complicated crisis, one that could not be resolved in a redemptive way quickly.

In this compounded tragedy, Kay faced serious life decisions previously incomprehensible to a young Christian mother. Medical specialists were pressing her to consider abortion. Thoughts of divorce, death, sickness, and shame pressed in on her and her heart constantly. But I found Kay to be a remarkable person. These pressures that would often drive people into isolation and bitterness, actually turned Kay to a Jesus who became her Peace, Comforter, Healer, Restorer, Counselor, and Guide. I bear witness that God Himself strongly supported her, giving her wisdom and counsel to assure good decisions while ministering to her deepest soul in the midst of all things passing. Imagine having to drill into your children never to use your bathroom, only their own. She had to develop all kinds of rules to safeguard the children's health—like never touching mommy's blood if she cut herself.

> **Kay faced serious life decisions previously incomprehensible to a young Christian mother.**

She faced the prospect of not seeing her children grow, not attending their school activities, not watching with pride as they graduated high school, went to college, married, had children. All the dreams a mother holds in her heart were dissolving under the weight of this heavy prognosis. Kay had scriptural grounds to divorce him outright. She could have become an embittered woman, mired in self-pity, harboring rage toward Joe and even the Lord for this horrible injustice. She could easily and understandably cut him out of her life and the children's lives. But she did not. And that was a choice, not her first feeling. Kay is an extraordinary woman who loves God and trusts Him. She drew near to the Lord and allowed Him to work forgiveness and wisdom into her heart.

Joe was a broken man. He was in shock, disoriented by the complete severing of virtually all of the relationships he had enjoyed with family and friends. He reckoned he would live with his mother as he slowly fell ill and ultimately died, alienated from his wife and children. The most important relationship we focused on was his relationship with Christ. He needed to know God still loved him, would forgive him, and not forsake him, even in death. Secondly, he had to commit to working on himself and his long-standing, secret struggle with homosexuality.

Joe was in crisis. He could not absorb the terrible repercussions of his actions all at once. It took time for him to let it in, feel it, grieve it. At first he thought that allowing himself to feel anything would be his undoing. But by summoning the courage and through humbling himself before the Lord, he was surprised to see how sweetly and deeply the Holy Spirit can help one to experience a genuine, deep, godly sorrow that became for Joe the foundation for his repentance and recovery.

At first Joe thought that allowing himself to feel anything would be his undoing.

Early on everyone who gives counsel in such an extreme situation must determine eventually the genuineness of sorrow. Is this repentance truly felt, is it deep? It may surprise some to know that often the client is so devastated by exposure, when the secret is suddenly revealed by outside circumstances, that the initial feelings and responses between godly sorrow and worldly sorrow are quite the same. However, genuine godly sorrow will always press on to a true repentance that is deep, exposing a contrite heart, not in just word, but in works, over time. But the dynamic here is that this nuclear family has been set up to shift into something other than what God wants for the husband of a woman, the father of children.

Let us start by saying this, you can truly forgive, and also see that the person is never to be trusted again. To work on reconciliation to the place of genuine forgiveness from one person to another, pastor, may often be all that you will ever accomplish, and that is itself a great work of God.

To go beyond that, beyond forgiveness to repatriation, is an entirely other matter. And this is what is so amazing about Joe and Kay's story. If they were to reconcile and restore their marriage, total honesty was absolutely required from Joe. No more lying, no more covering up, no more withholding. If she were ever to regain her trust in him, he would have to willingly submit to total accountability in all aspects of his life. Her decision to trust again could not be based upon her feelings. She needed to see genuine amendment of life.

Now back to that unhealthy shift I had warned against. This is a two-way street. A man and a woman are coming together to reestablish some normalcy in their family for their children's sake and theirs as well. It is not OK for one, considered to be the initial perpetrator, to live totally accountable in his life of genuine repentance, while the other partner never moves off being the warden of the relationship. Kids will more than notice that. And if that gets stuck, maybe it would have been honestly better to part, and to deal with those realities. Don't forget that when one human being hurts another, there is the first and initial hurt, but in every act of evil done, there is also the incredible temptation one begins in other's lives. It is the temptation to hate and to make the choice to not forgive. Actually, it is such a condition of the fallen human nature, that it is better said the other way. Just going with the flow of feelings about the injustice and harmfulness of things is all that is necessary to become *the warden*, and to never really forgive. To not hate, is the active choice, the choice we surely need God's help to accomplish. A line from one of my favorite movies poses the question from one man to another, "Did she forgive you?" "Yes," the other man answers, "A thousand times."

I hope the reader can see that this was truly a team effort. No *one* person could ever stand in the gap in such a situation where evil has struck out at so many people through all their interconnections.

No *one* person could ever stand in the gap in such a situation.

Husbands and wives throughout the church and the community are called to pray for this family. The minister here has his hands full. The counselor does as well. Accountability groups, support systems, not just for the adults in this story, but for the kids as well. Everyone needs to be attentive to one another. People are so vulnerable to believing the Lie at times like these. Pastor, call in the angels, heavenly ones and human ones as well. You have a people to disciple here, and there is many a Sunday, when everybody needs to hear that God loves them and will not forsake them.

I will never forget one particular day when I met with Kay. As she had prayed fervently for God's will, she came to believe that she had to choose a way to respond to her children's dad that would be best for them. Left to herself, without children, she admitted that she would likely have shut the door on him. She was tempted to strike out in revenge for the hurts and the devastation he had caused their family. I was listening to all of this, and then Kay said something I shall never forget, "How could small children see their family life so full of bitterness and resentment and still come to know and accept a loving heavenly Father?" After witnessing a sincere repentance in her husband, she knew she had to choose to begin the process of forgiveness, also instilling this attitude in their children. She voiced that this was not possible in human terms. By faith, she looked to God by whom all things are possible. It didn't happen overnight. She had to make an ongoing decision not to bring up the past, not to be the warden. She reminded herself that she didn't have rights of revenge. She chose to ask the Lord to help her control her tongue and her actions. It was not easy to forgive Joe but she boasts that the Lord supplied the grace.

"How could small children see their family life so full of bitterness and resentment and still come to know and accept a loving heavenly Father?"

Kay and Joe were separated for over two years. They prioritized their lives and together engaged in hundreds of hours of counseling, prayer, and hard work. In the midst of all that, they both decided to make concrete their reconciliation— against the wishes of some. Joe moved home on Valentine's Day. Don't think that doing God things God's way is ever easy, or without a downside at least in earthly circumstances. You have to choose the biggest right things, and often live with the rest. Again, even close family members who themselves love God, sometimes cannot abide your choices in God's path for you. How sad, but how real it often is. We surely are prone to forget that the tail end of Jesus' story of the prodigal returning is the added story of the elder brother's reaction. There were many issues that became topics of discussion in our counseling. I will list a few here:

❖ Kay's close relationship with her family
❖ The kids' putting pressure on Kay to have daddy move home
❖ The tension of Kay and the kids going to one church (her father's), and Joe going to another (the arrangement for more than five years)
❖ Their overall physical health and side effects from AZT usage and their fluctuating T-cell counts
❖ Their need for improved communication, recognizing the differences in each other that can often cause tension
❖ Shared responsibilities (child-rearing and household chores)
❖ Their sexual relationship and need for resensitization
❖ Mutual respect for one another's feelings and concrete ways of expressing that matter
❖ The ongoing issue of trust and accountability (reestablishing trust)
❖ Concerns about transmitting HIV to their four children (safety precautions)

> ❖ Dealing with the "grapevine" and inquisitiveness of people in this small town, and discussing mutually agreed upon conversational boundaries when talking to others
> ❖ Kay's fears that people would stop coming by once Joe moved back home
> ❖ Joe's need to be affirmed and appreciated for the right and good things he was doing

These are but a few of the many topics we covered during this time. Slowly I observed them redevelop ease with one another, better communication, and even slight but definite physical affection. Occasionally in ministry you have the rare privilege of taking part in a spiritual drama that leaves you in awe. Their story so leaves me. They are truly an exemplary witness to the power of God at work in human hearts. Not only were their hearts tested, hundreds of hearts were tested in the crucible of this crisis. I am writing this book 18 years after these events took place. I am grateful to report that all four children were spared being infected with the HIV virus. Joe and Kay have enjoyed the gift of raising their children and seeing each graduate from high school. Joe and Kay are in reasonably good health, living with HIV. I have known a number of people who died of AIDS-related diseases within a year of infection. God's hand, His work, His grace, mercy, and favor are evident in this family in a most profound way.

Beyond the workings of God in their lives, it must be emphasized that all along the way Joe, Kay, her family members, his family members, and their church members were faced with matters of the heart, and conscience.

Life asks us questions every day whether we recognize them or not. How did Jesus want Joe to respond to this crisis and everyone affected? How did Jesus want Kay to respond?

> **All along the way Joe, Kay, her family members, his family members, and their church members were faced with matters of the heart, and conscience.**

What questions were posed to the hearts of her parents, her siblings, her extended family and everyone in their church? This matter was not a closely controlled secret or a behind-the-scenes problem; it was a community event which played out for all to see.

I am dedicating another chapter to the pastoral need of discipleship to walk hand in hand with Christian counseling or reparative therapy. How critically important is the pastor's/minister's role in this team effort!

Ongoing Discipleship

I cannot overemphasize the great importance of ongoing discipleship in the successful treatment of persons struggling with homosexuality. As counselors, pastors, ministers, and caregivers, we must never lose sight of a tremendously important fact about the nature of the Kingdom of God.

One and part of all the politically correct ideologies of our day, including the attitudes and opinions

> **I cannot overemphasize the great importance of this part of the process.**

which are more and more being forced upon us by the tools of culture in our media, educational institutions, and entertainment, is the leveling to a common ground all the religions and mores of the peoples of the earth. They all have one thing in common, and in this they stand apart from Christendom. They all self-justify man's state before God, and define man as largely in no need for improvement. This is actually the mirror side of paganism, that man is free to create the idea of God in any way that pleases and self-justifies man. Christianity, alone claims absolute revelation as the source of the knowledge of God in Christ, indeed, that it is God who reveals himself, for our benefit. Only Christianity offers humanity the God-Man, Jesus, who exchanges His righteousness for our sin, and gives this grace to all who would believe and have faith in Him.

If you know Christ, I am absolutely confident you know this. This chapter is simply calling for the tremendous work of ongoing discipleship to continually emphasize these truths to your "client." He or she is seeking your help and guidance. In short, Jesus has the divine right to purchase and endow the identity of truly redeemed humanity upon His people, and to expect them to walk in that new reality. The church must proclaim, teach, and defend this gospel, or we will inadvertently leave it to the *gay* agenda to teach theirs.

In all my days of ministering, discipling, and counseling, I have never had a harder time getting the idea of repentance and grace, forgiveness and joy, into the head and heart of another, than when that person is struggling with sexual brokenness. Shame and despair are his constant companions. The Accuser never leaves his side. For these people, John 3:16 may speak of the great love God has for other people, but not them. Consequently, they are set up for a great self-deception. This is what is called the idealized other life. This principle is an easy one. The more obsessed and fixated clients are about a problem, the more "idealizing" they become about how great a life would be without that problem. This is also commonly seen in substance abuse cases where addictive tendencies are in place, including the abuse of drugs which produce psychotic episodes, mood altering episodes, and also the use of hallucinogens. It is the same with severe alcohol abuse as well. The clients project that if only they were not so "locked in" to things they believe are beyond their control, then they would have this perfect imagined life. "If only I did not have *this* problem, life would be great."

> **Shame and despair are constant companions.**

Sadly, it is simply not the case. In my life there have been some moments when I did not know how I would meet my obligations and pay my bills. There have been other moments when I have stood over the graves of those whom I thought would surely outlive me. I have had best friends betray me. I have also been at times, I am sure, a disappointment to others. Life isn't easy. If each person had a magic wand that would make all that he feels he suffers to go away, guess what, we are still sinners. We all have a life to live, with temptations and trials, with "fears within and foes without" (Hymn, "Just As I Am"). We still would need God's grace to live this life in Christ—end of story.

Let's now look at some specific ways in which those who struggle need the supportive work of discipleship and edification. First keep in mind that there is a greater goal for the person struggling with same-gender issues than the total elimination of homosexual attractions. This higher purpose is none other than being conformed into the image and likeness of Christ (Rom 8:29). The one who struggles with homosexuality experiences an inner conflict that is so pervasive that it takes on enormous proportions in their self-image, in their daily thought life, and in their life choices and actions. Most of my clients learned to wear masks very early in life. They made every effort to hide the "struggle," trying to keep it a carefully guarded secret. This became their new normality.

I can also say that most of my clients were raised in biblically centered, evangelical Christian church settings. Thus, this life of secrecy became a living hell fraught with shame, self-hatred, fear, anxiety, depression, despair, and hopelessness. They view their own homosexuality as the bane of their existence and source of all *secondary* problems in their lives. This is a grossly distorted perspective, but it is so real to them.

Most have asked God repeatedly to forgive their actual or imagined sins. They have not only prayed, many have begged God to take these thoughts and attractions away from them, almost always to no avail. They fall prey to a commonly held false assumption: that if this one huge problem would be resolved, their life would be simply wonderful. They think that were it not for this one debilitating predicament, they would be pretty swell folks. With the big "H" out of the picture God would begin to bless them, and they could begin to live a life they have idealized for years.

This becomes a vexing spiritual dilemma. If God judges homosexual acts as sinful and contrary to His will, why would He not answer a heartfelt request to deliver someone from this problem? This, I assure you, is a really hard one for them to understand. Remember, like all people in crisis, those struggling with homosexuality normally cannot live with such painful turmoil indefinitely. Something must give, and it does. Sadly, what often does give way is a vital and personal faith in Christ. Their conclusions, drawn from years of unanswered prayers, are frequently the wrong ones:

- ❖ God has rejected me, and there is no help or hope of my escaping this!
- ❖ God made me this way, and I need to find a church that affirms gay Christians.
- ❖ I have heard that the Bible does not condemn homosexuality, and so I am OK.
- ❖ I might as well face that this is the way God made me, and everyone else will just have to get used to it.

Most Christian leaders are not equipped to work through all of these issues with therapeutic interventions in order to help a person find his way. But listen, it is not primarily your job to do so. Christian discipleship is a great pastoral responsibility, and in a soul's redemption it is the foundation upon which a trained counselor or therapist can build. Nothing could overemphasize the importance of a Christian pastor and a community of loving Christians whose faith is centered on Jesus and who understand the power of the gospel. There are major biblical themes and sound principles of faith that must be reintroduced to these persons, for they have clearly forgotten them, or were never taught them in the first place. These truths have been under great attack within what is left of their reason. To say it more clearly, without the basis of faith in the absolutes of God's love and God's Word, the counselor has more than two strikes against him or her before he even gets to the plate.

Remember, as discussed earlier, that same-gender attractions (SGA) have little to do with sex in the beginning. If you have young clients struggling with gender confusion, then you can normally assume that they have a gender deficit that needs to be addressed as early as possible. Failing this, they are vulnerable to eroticizing these attractions with the onset of puberty. Most of these individuals who have experienced SGA since childhood or early adolescence are at risk of "sexualizing" their identity. They are in a process of, or have already come to the conclusion that they

Same-gender attractions have little to do with sex in the beginning.

are gay. They ultimately make what seems to them to be a logical judgment that in truth is not the result of good logic. They risk concluding that the same-gender attraction they have experienced for years defines, even proves, who they are as persons. This then becomes a *sexualized identity*— a false identity, a fallen identity. Timing is critical in the formation of God's word within the heart of our children. They need good, solid, biblical teaching starting with the material in the early Genesis record—the creation of Man, male and female in God's image.

Again, this is where we begin to understand God's creative purpose for human sexuality. Homosexuality is a distortion of God's intent. Within our Judeo-Christian worldview is the belief that we cannot know who we are apart from God's revelation. The Word of God is our reference point, not our feelings. Subjective creatures are not better than their Creator in establishing their own identity. An individual who embraces a homosexual identity has himself believed a lie. It can be an honest conclusion based upon their personal experience.

From the outset of my working with people who struggle with homosexuality, I have sought to redirect their sense of self. These wonderful yet troubled persons need to discover a higher view of who they truly are in Christ according to the Word of God. The Bible above all other sources provides the only sure foundation upon which we can come to understand our true identity and our created purpose.

> **These wonderful yet troubled persons need to discover a higher view of who they truly are in Christ.**

Everyone has a belief system that largely guides their behavior. Part of the task of a pastor, minister, counselor in the work of discipleship is to "ferret out the lie" that twists and distorts the true nature of one's self-identity. This is essential if we are going to be able to assist others in correcting distorted perceptions of their own nature and therefore their view of God. This is not a step you can skip. As Proverbs 23:7 states: "For as he thinks within himself, so he is" (NASB). The individual struggling with homosexuality will sabotage their own Christian growth and process of maturity and sanctification, repeatedly, until a number of core erroneous beliefs are altered, and replaced with God's truth and love.

The Bible provides abundant material covering God's view of man's heart. The heart is used as a figure for man's inner personal life. It contains the real us, our true character. Jesus emphasized that it is our heart God wants, and it is our hearts that He wants to transform—not just our outer behaviors. Scripture makes it abundantly clear that a radical change must occur in our thought life in order that a work of metamorphosis or "transformation" might take place. And it is in this work that we participate with the Holy Spirit wherein we may come to receive and embrace the mind of Christ (Rom 8:5; 1 Cor 2:16; Phil 2:5; 1 Pet 4:1). Paul exhorts us to be proactive in this work of renewing our minds (Rom 12:2-3; Eph 4:23). As mentioned above, we are not alone in this process of sanctification. The Holy Spirit is at work in this renewal (Ps 51:10; Isa 41:1; 2 Cor 4:16; Phil 1:6; Col 3:10; Titus 3:5).

One assignment I give most of my clients is to pray Paul's prayers in Eph 1:12-19b and Eph 3:14-21 (see the preface page at the beginning of this book). I ask them to personalize these prayers, asking the Lord for these results in their own lives. And I suggest that they pray these prayers at least once daily for a month, for so much of what they truly need can only come by way of revelation in their hearts by the Word of God and action of the Holy Spirit.

> **One assignment I give most of my clients is to pray Paul's prayers in Ephesians and personalize them.**

I also utilize a number of allegorical metaphors along the way in the initial phase of my work with clients. Our Lord is truly a master teacher. His stories have a way of lodging in the imagination—these metaphors are ones that people can easily remember and carry with them. I will share two with you that I have found over the years to be exceptionally beneficial in my counseling. The first addresses how they perceive their ongoing struggle with homosexuality. The second addresses their thought life.

Most Christians who come to me for counseling have experienced their homosexuality as though it were a rabid pit bull that relentlessly chases them through life. They are running as fast as they can to escape the beast, for they know that if they ever halt their panicked flight, this creature will devour them. When I share this image and ask if this is how they feel, almost without exception I hear, "Exactly!" They have viewed their attractions as their mortal enemy, and themselves as stuck in an endless cycle of fight or flight. "What if these attractions are not an enemy, but a friend?" I ask. The very idea seems totally ridiculous to them.

Then I ask them to consider a reframe as a tool in their efforts to win this battle. "I want you to begin to think of these attractions as a teacher, a mentor, a guide trying to get your attention in order to help you gain insight about your self, your past, and your life journey. Consider that this is their effort to reveal to you things regarding your family system, your childhood and adolescent development. These feelings you have thought of as temptations can actually illumine your legitimate and normal 'relational needs' and perhaps reveal some ways you were deprived or wounded." This normally gets their interest because it is so opposite of how they have previously thought about SGA.

> **I ask them to think of these attractions as a teacher helping them to gain insight.**

When I speak in churches, I often say, "People didn't ask for or choose these attractions; they were just there." They did not understand the origin or nature of them—where they came from or what they meant. Eventually, they sexualized the attractions and came to a faulty conclusion as to what they meant: *I must be gay*. Those attractions largely have to do with what is or is not evolving in their family relationships, gender identification, personal experiences, and self-perception. The attractions point the way and can help provide the trained counselor with the insight to locate and identify the origin and development of the person's problem of gender confusion. This of course is necessary in their progress toward healing and growth.

The second allegorical metaphor I use is *The Radio*. It came to me one afternoon after a conversation with my 89-year-old grandmother. For most of us, a common radio is nothing extraordinary, but it was to my grandparents who were born in the 1890s. In their lifetime they transitioned from outhouses to indoor plumbing, wells to public water, oil lamps to modern lighting, and the list is endless.

Radios—what an amazing invention! You turn it on and begin turning the other dial and immediately, scores of different stations provide every genre of music, sports, news, and commentary imaginable. How? Well, as you sit reading this book, untold numbers of radio waves, invisible to the naked eye, surround you. You cannot see them but they are real nonetheless. Everywhere you go they are there, whether you think of them or not. This intriguing invention was designed to be a *receiver* of transmissions. The waves enter into the radio, are processed, and then broadcast in a way we can hear. The radio is not the original source of the wave transmission; it simply receives from a wider spectrum, and makes them audible to us. The broadcast message, or music, comes to us from an outside source and enters into our thoughts and mind through our physical hearing. When I share the radio metaphor with clients, I bring it down to this point. As Paul states clearly, "Our struggle is not against flesh and blood, but against the rulers, against the powers, against the spiritual forces of wickedness in the heavenly places," (Eph 6:11-16), and we're exhorted to put on the full armor of God to be able to stand firm against their schemes.

The radio simply receives from a wider spectrum, and makes them audible to us.

This reframe reminds the client that not all their thoughts were of their own making, and many of the messages and urges are from outside influences. These thoughts are not original; we weren't the source, but thoughts from the outside, once inside, can influence us for good or evil. People are too quick to assume all thoughts are their own. Christians should have a larger paradigm.

I often reflect that when the Lord told us that he himself tempts no man, that the assumption would then be that temptations come from an outside source. Why else would God remind us of that disclaimer? Jesus said, "My sheep will hear My voice." The apostle John wrote: *"He who has an ear, let him hear what the Spirit says to the churches"* (Rev. 3:22). We were created to hear the voice of our Lord, and that is a truly wondrous matter. Would that his was the only voice we are capable of hearing. Just as there are hundreds of invisible radio waves that surround us, there is a profound, unseen reality.

The enemy is very tactical in his planning the destruction of a human person. It seems that the evil one would stop at nothing to debase us and would do everything possible to cause us to become distracted in our relationship with God. These messengers of darkness will work to instill distorted thinking, confusion, and falsehood, drawing us away from Truth and distancing us, in our perceptions from the love of God. They will make every effort to bring about disillusionment, to cause us to suffer and to despair of even our faith. Remember, that in their secret life these persons have already begun to isolate themselves from God's faithful people. The enemy's purpose, of course, is our eventual and complete destruction.

I often recommend the reading of the *Screwtape Letters* by C.S. Lewis. It's a humorous, thought-provoking correspondence between two devils as the higher-in-rank demon mentors the underling in how best to ensnare and hurt the Christian. Then I ask my clients, "Does every thought that whirls around in your head originate with you, or is it possible that some of those thoughts originate from a source outside of you and are suggested to you?" What about many guys I work with who at a young age heard thoughts (voices) inside them saying, "You're **Our minds are a great, vast battleground.** gay. You were born this way. You can't change. This is who you are." My point is this: our minds are a great, vast battleground. Hence, when Jesus was asked the question about the greatest commandment, his response included the phrase: *"You shall love the Lord with all your mind."*

Why would Paul tell us to take every thought captive to Christ? What does he mean when he says, *"Guard your hearts and minds in Christ Jesus?"* If we're not discerning, we can hear suggestions made so subtly, with such stealth, that we assume them our own. These thoughts that we think are our own, lead us to conclude that this is how we must truly "feel" about the matter. The thoughts may frighten us, they may tempt us, and they could injure us in a variety of ways if we allow them a place in our hearts and then choose to act upon them.

Don't get me wrong; man himself is certainly capable of his own debased thoughts and passions. Nonetheless, we are bombarded with many voices, impulses, and temptations throughout our lives. The spiritual battlefield is both for and within our minds. I implore my clients struggling with homosexuality to grow in Christ. I encourage them to become deeply grounded in the Word of God, and if they had strayed from it, to return, and thus to grow again in spiritual discernment so that they can take captive to Christ every thought that issues forth from the works of the devil.

Again, focus on discipleship, build your people, build up their faith, teach the Word of God, and illumine His words in the minds of those you counsel. And pastors, never forget to pray for those you disciple and encourage. God is your partner, and you need Him to win this battle. As Luther said, "Were not the right Man on our side, our striving would be losing!"

Clinical Thoughts and Tools:
An Assessment Guide

The Dirty Jobs and Dark Places
Appeals to Be Ecumenical in Our Common Survival
Right to Privacy: The Last Stand for the Church
Final Comments and Challenges

This chapter on *Assessment Guides and Tools*, is an attempt to offer a complement to what you have already developed as a caregiver/pastor-minister. Do not take this chapter as inclusive of all you need, but rather parallel to all that you use at a professional level in the care of souls.

Do not neglect the basics. There is already published in this series by College Press an introductory guide to counseling fundamentals—[*A Shepherd's Guide to Counseling Fundamentals* (Caring for the Flock) by Beth Robinson]. This and other fine works like it give you an excellent review on important bases to touch, a good glossary of terms in the more clinical world of counseling, and overviews of concepts basic to counseling approaches.

Don't forget that in dealing with homosexual issues, most of your clients who reach out for help are in crisis. Remember that the crises specific to this primer on homosexuality are usually event driven, but overlap heavily with developmental life transitions, identity crisis through adolescence, family systems, and transgenerational family dysfunction. Some will approach you because they are struggling with the long-range effects of overt acts of sexual abuse. If things were not complicated enough, you are also dealing with the wrapping of an exterior culture which is in a major moral shift, with all the entrapments and messages of Hollywood and sexually based advertising models as much driven to create a market as capture one that already exists.

On top of these matters mentioned above, you have an Enemy who has already begun to erode the personal identity of the soul you care for. This I.P. (the identified patient, or the identified problem) sitting in your office is very confused, and has shifted in the knowledge of who he is as a human being, from his/her being created by God, and redeemed by Christ, into something the world wants them to be, which I assure you is not a healthy, whole, integrated human personality.

Lastly, as a pastor, you must never forget your role to first be their shepherd, their minister, and their ambassador for Christ. Please do not stray far from your pastoral model, into the world of the therapist. I assure you, doing that will often negatively affect your ability to be their minister and—perhaps most important—their spiritual father. There are roles in families that are of God, and they are important. There are things Mom can do that Dad cannot, and the opposite is true as well. Fathers have a unique role in calling the child at a certain age away from the mother, not to the father, but to stand on his or her own legs, as dad names the good in them and calls them to adulthood in Christ. This is for daughters as well as sons. Can moms in single parent families do this? She can try, and that is better than nothing, but just as nothing can replace mom in certain ways, nothing can replace dad in fundamental ways as well.

> **Please do not stray far from your pastoral model, into the world of the therapist.**

Pastor, in the spiritual family of your church, I am sure you are aware of how many souls look to you as their spiritual dad. They need *you*, and if you are reading this book for some immediate concern, that one lamb may really need you now.

In this chapter you are going to see a guide to be used as a checklist as you do an intake assessment. These listings of words and questions are meant to assist you in identifying what may be important patterns or discoveries. Some of the questions you ask may stimulate a good bit of responsive conversation with the client. Some may not. But watch for the ones that give you the nonverbal responses, or the quick dismissals, ones that may create a certain tension in the room.

Remember, it is not often wise to discover something and rip it open. Things are scabbed over for a reason, there is a sore spot under there, and it is always better that sensitive information is volunteered rather than for you to go "exploring." Having been in these situations all my professional life, I know how difficult it can be when young clients are dragged into your office, having been exposed by some circumstance or event, and feeling like they would rather be on Mars than in this circumstance. You must protect them! Give them comfort, de-escalate the emotional pain, put a salve on their impulsive factors, and try to begin building some trust during these initial moments. This, of course, is not the time to use the following guide or your own intake interview. Take care of the person. Ask permission to let you help: to face and to work through problems with the help of God, the loving Father of us all.

Assessment Guide Supplement

If you can get the IPs to tell you their story — LISTEN well,
and half of these questions may be answered, even before you have to ask.

Are any of the following listed in the presenting problems?

Alcohol Use Disorder	Eating Disorders
Prescription Drug Abuse	Attempts at Suicide
Amphetamine/Cocaine Abuse	Manic Episodes
Opiate Use	Bipolar Disorder
Generalized Anxiety	Attention Deficit Disorder
Passive/Aggressive	Histrionic Personality
Narcissistic Personality	Sadistic/Masochistic Personality
Phobias	Sexual Addiction
Borderline Personality	Paraphilias NOS
	(not otherwise specified)

Are there any sexual disorders mentioned, such as:

Fetishes	Transvestite behavior	Transgender confusion
Exhibitionism	Voyeurism	Sexual masochism/sadism
Zoophilia	Gender identity disorder	Frotteurism
Pedophilia	Ephebophilia	

Overall Physical Health: What diagnosed physical conditions are present (diabetes, heart disease, cancer, etc)?

What medications is the person taking (scripted or non-scripted)? Be sure to question their purpose as well as looking for interaction factors. For example, almost all drugs given for psychological purposes or for pain do not do well with alcohol.

Inventory of Past Family Relationships/Expectations
Areas of Possible Concerns

Have client list expectations and/or beliefs regarding males, male roles, male boundaries, etc. in their family of origin—all male roles including dad, dad as husband, uncles, brothers, and smaller male children.

List similar expectations and/or beliefs regarding females in your family of origin.

Females: Do they have appropriate boundaries? Could you have boundaries in relationship with them? As above, regard all female roles including mom, mom as wife, aunts, sisters, and smaller female children.

❖ Parent history: Alive? Married? Separated? Divorced? Remarried?

❖ Raised by a single parent? Are all your siblings full siblings?

❖ Relationship with *father* (biological, adopted, step-father).

❖ Relationship with *mother* (biological, adopted, step-mother).

❖ What were the stated rules of the relationships in your home?

❖ What were the real rules, meaning who had power and who did not?

Ask clients to imagine a large room with a big banquet table set for thirty people, then ask them in their family (of five?), where everyone would sit at a typical meal. You do this to help them measure emotional distance. Devise other ways to help them communicate the reality of their home during their childhood/adolescence that might help the client put into words or pictures information you are seeking, memories or info that needs to be looked at.

Bullet Points for males and females struggling with homosexual issues:

For male clients:

Father Void One: Vacuum, father not present, or absent emotionally. This must be substantive and quantitative.

Father Void Two: Father is a negative presence, harsh, overly rigid, unable to model the strong, but warmhearted father.

Mother Presence One: Mother present and is domineering, extremely strong-willed, and perhaps blaming.

Mother Presence Two: Mother is present and overly affectionate to the son, inappropriate transference of affection from husband to son, symbiotic.

Listen for Indicators Authority figures and/or nearby family members who have seriously crossed boundaries, incestuous acts or postures, either in the nuclear or the extended family. These can be uncles, older brothers, close family friend, previous pastor, teacher, school counselor, etc.

The I P (Teenage):
(The identified person) Look for changes in peers and lifestyle: evidence of drugs, absence or avoidance of long-term friends, change of dress, language, depreciation of other's boundaries, secretive, changes in music, appetite, grades, comments from teachers, behavioral problems, dissociative.

For Female Clients:

Father Presence One: Father is a negative presence, harsh, overly rigid, unable to model the strong, but warmhearted father.

Father Presence Two: Father presence may be more of an absentee father, and especially in a way that projects abandonment where male is seen as one who will not protect and treasure females.

Father Presence Three: Father is more rigid in gender roles, his own as well as wife's and daughter's; abusive sexually in a degrading way, or perhaps in a symbiotic manner, transferring affection from wife to daughter. Any or combinations of these to the end that there is left a real hatred of men or fear of men. This may be initially communicated as great indifference.

Mother Presence One: An emotional void, or detachment in relationship with daughter. Not so much a truly negative force as a vacuum, or a somewhat strained relationship leaving a need for mother bonding, attachment, etc.

Nuclear Family/Peers: During childhood and adolescence, leaving a void in sense of self as feminine or as a feminine being. Goals of adolescence and identity formation are not achieved. Enters late adolescence without any sense of belonging either in groups or especially in family.

Listen for Indicators Male figures who have seriously crossed boundaries, incest—either in the nuclear or extended family. Again, these can be uncles, older brothers, close family friends, past or present pastor, teacher(s), school counselor, etc. Check this out with female figures as well. Listen for indicators that there was a lack or void of female relationships altogether. What about girlfriends, peers, groups or clubs? To what extent is the person socially involved? This can be very revealing about their sense of self in relation to others, a sense of belonging, of being connected—or not.

Before we continue with the rest of this assessment tool, let me preface it with a story from a friend who has ministered in another state and has served the church for many years. During his early college experience, one of his fellow students was working his way through school, ministering in a small town a few miles from an institute where they were studying.

A man in this congregation, a farmer, who possessed a rigid and paranoid personality, discovered that his fourteen-year-old daughter was pregnant. Enraged, the father berated her and his two sons as well to get them to say who it was that got his girl pregnant. The boys claimed ignorance. The girl, red-faced with shame, unable to look at her dad, would not speak.

The man put the daughter in the cab of his old pickup and told the boys to climb in the back. He proceeded to drive through every street of this small community, yelling loudly from the truck, house to house, angrily demanding to know who got his girl pregnant. Imagine how the girl felt with her father behaving this way. It almost sounds like a scene right out of the film, *To Kill A Mockingbird*. That night, the father, unrelenting in his intense interrogation, finally discovered that it was his own two boys who had gotten their sister pregnant. They had been taking her sexually since she was about ten years old. When she entered puberty, she finally became pregnant. About this time in the story, one of the elders, a friend of the farmer, asked the young college-aged minister to call on the family.

What is the point of my telling this story? My main purpose is to illumine that dirty jobs sometimes need to be done, and they often fall onto the lap of pastors and counselors. Sometimes, someone must have to look in the dark places. It can be odious and a bit scary. It is certainly a place to tread lightly, for you are treading in the deep recesses of a person's heart and memories.

I don't know the rest of that story, but, let us roll the clock ahead twenty years and wonder if there may be a middle aged married woman in your church who now struggles with lesbianism. Maybe she wants to end her marriage, and maybe she has never bonded with her two sons that she has borne into this world. In a normal intake interview process, this one little untold tidbit of her past, may never be unburied, or spoken, but will remain forever hidden in a shame so very deep. It may be that the past has never been revealed since the day that young pregnant girl dropped out of high school as a freshman and later went on to marry the first boy who would have her just to escape her father's house. There may be a baby in her past that she never held in her arms, and that she was forced to give away. It may also be that she has never developed a good attitude toward men in general, and a worse one about herself. It may be that she has a hard time relating to God as Father. Maybe she thinks she is a lesbian today, still hurting, still confused and still hiding things in dark places. But if she is willing to let it happen, seeking help for herself would be a most courageous act. She will likely need someone to go into the dark places with her, and turn on the light of truth and the love of Jesus. Someone who would take the time to show some compassion and to build some trust, and who would ask her permission to carry the flashlight, just might have some success. I hope this story helps us remember that Jesus has asked us to help people, and not to be too quick in our judgment of them.

What follows includes a list of dark places and possible circumstances that are often part of the story of some very damaged and vulnerable people.

Exploring Nuclear Family Relationships and Potential Issues

List all siblings (gender, age, birth order), and describe your relationship with each.

Genogram literature and software can be very helpful in your assessment of family dynamics. If used correctly, it can lift a great deal of personal shame off of the individual client, who is struggling with deep emotional pain. (See annotated bibliography at end of this book.)

❖ How was conflict dealt with in the family (avoidance, denial, expression and dialogue, suppression)? Generally were matters worked through to a healthy resolution? Was there a parent who could never be wrong? Were there often situations where someone would be loud, blaming, and angry, rather than see "themselves at fault" or take personal responsibility?

❖ Divorce? Remarriage? Step-siblings? Multigenerational home (grandparent or other relative living with family)? Did a single mom with a drug problem raise the client? Were there multiple paramours (live-in companions)? Was the mom a prostitute?

❖ Did your client experience foster care as a child, and if so was he or she ever physically or sexually abused while in the custody of the state?

❖ Does your client—male or female—experience any of the symptoms of separation anxiety? Did either of your client's parents in their childhood?

❖ How was love expressed in the family? Were there ever actions, words, or gifts that expressed love and value of a person? Were these gifts appropriate?

❖ Was love expressed freely and often?

❖ Would the client say their family was intimate and healthy or distant and emotionally detached?

❖ In a Family-System model, were there healthy rhythms of "closeness" followed by healthy "distancing," only to repeat itself? Or, were things stuck in closeness or in distance to achieve equilibrium?

- ❖ What was it like growing up in your family?
  Look for intergenerational patterns (alcoholism, suicide, abuse, divorce, out-of-wedlock children, severe problems with boundaries, etc).
- ❖ Are there key family members from whom you are estranged? (Parent, Sibling, Grandparent, Uncle, Aunt, or Cousins)
- ❖ Your parents' relationship as you perceived it growing up (affectionate, conflictual, intimate, distant, abusive—verbally or emotionally)
  Physical Abuse?
  Sexual Abuse?
  Emotional Abuse?
- ❖ Nuclear family secrets (e.g., suicide, imprisonment, mental illness, pedophilia, illegitimacy, abortion, financial failures, abuse, previous marriage, incest, etc.)
- ❖ Who was closest to your dad of you and your siblings?
- ❖ Who was closest to your mom of you and your siblings?
- ❖ Who did your mom seem to focus on the most?
- ❖ Who did your dad seem to focus on the most?

Exploring certain childhood social factors:

❖ List any significant early childhood memories.

❖ Would you describe yourself in early childhood as being a loner?

❖ Who were your peer groups/friends?

❖ Did you have many/few friends or total lack thereof (this is especially important in SGA)

❖ Were you in any clubs? If yes, were they a substitute for more intimate friendships?

❖ What role did you play in sports? Any positive or negative memories associated with that experience?

Gym and locker rooms   School showers
School buses   Detentions, purpose
Detentions, rooms   School bathrooms
Certain teachers   Playgrounds
Before/after school

❖ Was there any cruel teasing or name calling growing up?

❖ How did you feel about your physical body in early to middle childhood? In high school?

❖ Was that a major factor in your personality development, and in your friendships or lack of them?

❖ When you were a kid, did you ever lock yourself in a bathroom, closet, or your bedroom at night?

❖ Most kids like a light on at night, why did you?

❖ Did you have as a child any obsessive fears, some thing or some place that you avoided at all costs, or that made you extremely uncomfortable? Did you have then some place or some thing that made you feel safe?

❖ Did you play with dolls as a child? With animals? And do you ever remember anything about your play that you reflect on now as untoward or unusual? Do you remember anyone playing with you in an untoward manner?

❖ Did you in your middle childhood years still have problems with bed-wetting? Controlling defecation at school?

❖ Did you play with fire or intentionally hurt yourself in physical ways? Fire alarms?

❖ Did you as a child have any imaginary friends? Describe them, and what do you think their purpose was in how they related to you or you to them? Were there animals among your imaginary friends, such as horses, or lions, etc.? Did you have repeated death dreams? Was there a sexual nature to any of them?

❖ Listen for any indication that a child's behavior or sexual understanding seemed very advanced for their years—even if you are listening to a teenage or adult client describe their childhood.

Warning: Do not attempt to intervene quickly in the lives of smaller children whose behaviors may indicate trauma of some nature, physically or sexually. Call for professional help. Many times early intervention with smaller children is later seen as either planting an idea, devaluing later testimony, or, is in itself a furthering of the trauma of the child. The purpose of this book is a primer for caregivers who work with teens who are confused in their adolescence, and for those struggling on through adult years.

Nudity in the Home

❖ Did an opposite gender parent dress and undress in front of you? Up through what age?

❖ Was this level of familiarity (nudity) treated naturally and casually, or did family members respect boundaries by undressing behind the privacy of a closed door?

❖ Do you remember whether normal parental acts such as bathing a child or dressing that child exceeded fairly normal seasons when such acts would be handed over and some privacy respected, usually during the middle childhood years and on into preteen years?

❖ Did you ever see your parents involved in intimate sexual behavior?

❖ Were you ever told that your parent had wanted the opposite gender child when you were born?

Pornography

1. **Have you ever looked at pornography?**
   Do you recall your first encounter with pornography?
2. **Did you discover it on your own? In what context? What circumstance?**
   If introduced to you, by whom? What age?
   What has been your experience with pornography since?
3. **What is the most common type of pornography that you are drawn to?**
   ❖ What gender?
   ❖ What age range?
   ❖ What sexual act(s) are most compelling?
4. **Do you masturbate while looking at pornography?**
5. **How do you use your imagination while masturbating?**
6. **How frequently do you look at pornography?**
7. **How frequently do you masturbate?**
8. **Do any of the fetish groups have power over your imagination and your erotic responses?**
9. **Have you engaged in on-line chat rooms centered on sexual conversation?**
10. **Where is your computer(s) located?**
11. **Do you have or have you used an Internet filter designed to block pornography?**
12. **Do you have an accountability partner?**

WrapUp Conversations should then further explore

Attention: By this time into the counseling relationship, you should have known your client's patterns sufficiently to spot voids in his confessed behavior. For example, let's say you pose a question about the use of the imagination during masturbation, and your client becomes nervous, or cannot look you in the eyes. Perhaps his answer is vague, and you suspect there is more to say. There is obviously a need for clarification. Here are some prompts:

1. Have you actually connected with people you met in chat rooms?
2. Have you engaged in extramarital sexual activity? Are you at present? (Male? Female?)

3. Have you gone to parks or other public places to view or engage similar activities?

Prompts if you suspect minors are involved:

1. Have you ever had sex with a minor? This includes inappropriate touching, fondling, petting, kissing, groping, or any kind of an insertion whatsoever?
2. Have you fondled young children while sitting on your lap?
3. Have you parked near schoolyards or gone to little league games for other purposes than baseball?
4. Do you keep digital files or photos of young children engaged in any kind of sexual act, or who are unclothed?
5. Do you frequent parks in the evening that are known for such activities?

Please pay attention to the section later in this chapter regarding the mandated reporting of sex crimes and sexual child abuse.

Sexual History

Disclaimer—Please pay special attention:

Be reminded that if you do not live in the unique world of the Christian or professional counselor, then the use of assessment guides may be foreign to you. These are not individual points of discussion that every client needs to address. These guides are tools (an in-your-lap reminder or prompt) as interviews are taking place. Some who read this primer are already very skilled in the intake process and know its place between the de-escalation of crisis, and the beginning of the therapeutic process.

If you are not going to be the person who does the main work of counseling, then you would not be the person using this intake assessment tool. If you are doing the counseling, it will be easy to note the salient points of a client's story against one of the prompts below. His sharing such personal information usually comes in the form of a story, his own story. It is my intent to offer these guides as a supplement to the ones you are already using. I hope it helps. Also, a large percentage of your clients may have nothing to gain by addressing such a complete sexual history. Be sensitive, questioning heavily in nonrelated sexual matters, would likely push the client to doubt the altruism of the counselor.

Finally, as in triage, first do no harm. Sadly, too many people are in counseling for all the wrong reasons. Let me say this bluntly. America has become a nation of voyeurs. Too many counselors find themselves vulnerable to being such a voyeur into the shame and sexual brokenness of others. Such use of any of the materials in this book is counter to the intended purpose. This primer is a small attempt to bring any and all resources to bear in this great battle for souls. Please do not be offended, I tell you I question myself constantly as to my own motives in ministry, and I highly recommend that to others as well.

Then why do a sexual history? Well, simply put, that is the very area where the client's same-gender behavior is rooted. Remember, part of the counseling effort is to roll back the clock, find the damage, and correct the interpretations and conclusions made so long ago by the child, that is now the man or woman in your office in great pain. Help these souls, disciple them, and tell them that they are more normal in their human needs than they have ever believed themselves to be. Then roll up your sleeves and help them find some answers. And tell them Jesus loves them.

Sexual History

1. At what age did you begin puberty?
2. What age do you consider to be your sexual awakening?
3. Were you an early or late bloomer?
4. Males: when did you experience wet dreams, and how did you "relate" about that to your parents, other siblings, etc. How did you think or feel about the experience of them?
5. Females: when did you notice breast development, menstruation, and did you have any especially shame-based moments during that time.
6. Have you ever engaged in sexual experimentation growing up? At what age(s)?
   What behaviors, with what gender(s)?
   Mutual masturbation

Clinical Thoughts and Tools — 99

Mutual exploration
- ❖ Petting, kissing
- ❖ Oral sex, hand sex
- ❖ Heterosexual intercourse
- ❖ Anal sex, Fetishes, rituals

7. What feelings have you experienced after engaging in this sexual behavior?

❖ Shame	❖ Guilt	❖ Self-hatred
❖ Depression	❖ Anxiety	❖ Fear
❖ Panic	❖ Peace	❖ Comfort
❖ Relief	❖ Happiness	❖ Sadness
❖ Anger	❖ Suicidal	❖ Bitter
❖ Dirty	❖ Lonely	❖ Confused
❖ Hopeless	❖ Indifferent	❖ Self-Justifying
❖ Dissociative	❖ Powerful	❖ Giddy

Did you experience a manic phase either before or after such experiences?

Did you experience a depressive phase either before or after such experiences?

Were there events or circumstances in your life before these occurrences where you felt especially emasculated or impotent?

Did you notice feeling angry or especially frustrated just before these sexual activities?

8. Are there any meds you take, or are there other drugs you take that you have noticed leave you especially vulnerable to impulsive activities?

9. Are there other behaviors you struggle with such as gambling or taking extreme physical risks?

10. Are any of these behaviors done in an especially public way?

11. Do you ever use drugs or alcohol as a prelude to sex?

12. Has your sexual life taken on a "life of its own"?

13. Do you hide aspects of your sexual life from parents, spouse, or from others?

14. Do you in any way live a double sexual life?

15. If you have a hidden sex life of any kind, as a married person, does your spouse complain in any regard about your mutual sex life? Specifically, _____?

16. If your client has been acting out sexually, has he mentioned aspects of his behavior that seem more like predation, rather than dating or courting?

17. If your client has been acting out sexually, ask him if there is anyone in the background using or soliciting sex for purposes of blackmail or manipulation. Ask if your client is doing this to others.

18. If this is a boy/girl, a teen, or young college student, ask if others have used him or her for prostitution, either for money or through blackmail. If you suspect that this is a possibility, ask if any other member of the client's family has been threatened.

19. Has the male client struggling with homosexual issues ever involved one of his siblings in his behavior? Have siblings ever been involved in a sexual way with others?

20. Has the Internet ever been used to seek out relationships with minors/adults?

STDs

1. Have you ever been tested for sexually transmitted diseases?
2. Ever been diagnosed with an STD? Which one(s)?
3. Treatment? Status?

Incest

| Father | Mother | Brother/Sister | Cousin |
| Uncle/Aunt | Grandparent | Paramour | |

Sexual Molestation

❖ Family member/Stepfather or mother
❖ Friend of the family
❖ Teacher/Coach
❖ Clergy or youth leader
❖ School counselor
❖ Stranger

Age?   Nature of the abuse?
Extent?   Frequency/Duration?
Was this accompanied by:
        ❖ Verbal threat of harm to you or family members?
        ❖ Physical harm and pain?

> ❖ Fear, terror?
> ❖ Pleasure?
> ❖ Confusion?
> ❖ Was this reported? If so, what was the outcome?
> ❖ How did you feel after this experience?
> 25. Did a parent or older sibling dress you in opposite gender clothing as a child?
> 26. Look for signs of emotional dependency in your client's description of relationships.
> 27. Listen for possible evidence of a more *covert* or *emotional* type of incest, or abuse.

It is not uncommon to discover an enmeshed relationship between a parent and child, even if they are now both adults and on in years. This is particularly common between mothers and sons, where the son is struggling with homosexuality. Often these mothers are lacking fulfillment in their marriages and find comfort, understanding, attention, and affection from their sons. This is an unhealthy, dysfunctional dynamic. This client will need professional help in these circumstances. I have suggested excellent reading on this subject in the annotated bibliography.

Note: As you use this assessment guide, please remember that one of the main purposes is to stimulate the client to offer information. If you come to a place where the client begins to share openly, *do not interrupt for clarification!* It is far better to let the person move through all that he wants to say, especially on the initial occasion of speaking part of his story. That is a major breakthrough, and in sales lingo, a real buying signal. Here the client is starting to trust you with the "secret life," with the story. Be very aware of your own effect. Do not look shocked! Do make an effort to demonstrate some nonverbal compassion and understanding. Do not sit with a closed body posture. Keep eye contact within norms. Do not interrupt momentary pauses of up to a minute or more. Do not be uncomfortable with silence. In these circumstances the clients are probably weighing how much more they want to say. Later, or even on other occasions, you can ask for clarification where needed, or ask them to speak more on the matter as to how those things described made them feel.

These are just the basics of listening skills, but you would be surprised how a zealous interviewer can force the client to "clam up" by what is perceived by the client as an intrusive manner, increasing his or her own sense of vulnerability.

Big Problems, Big Job, Big Challenges

There is an enemy in the land, and he is after our sons and our daughters, our men, our women, and our children. He is after our rights and freedoms as Christians. He is after the integrity of the human and specifically the Christian family. And think about this, the Enemy does not care one bit if we are Baptists, Catholics, Pentecostals, Presbyterians, Methodists, Independent Non-Denominational Evangelicals, or Church of Christ. The Enemy wants us all to shut up about the Bible, about morals, and especially about God. I am so hopeful that in this time of Christian history, we might put some things, albeit important things, aside for a season, and start working together for the survival of us all. I do not mean to negate differences that are very important discussions. I am saying that we are being attacked at a level that is common to all Christians, and the times are calling this to be a top priority.

Please, please, consider the following: In the story I related above about the young minister during his seminary days, there is a question begging to be asked. If God has called you to be a minister in the more Protestant/Evangelical world in either the denominational, or the nondenominational brotherhoods, independent groups or otherwise, you are very vulnerable to the Enemy as you care for souls. The question involves the right to privacy versus laws in the land for mandated reporters of crimes, especially of children.

If you serve on the Catholic side of Christendom, as a priest, with a confessional, or if you use one of the forms of the Rite of Reconciliation that can be found in several of the Christian traditions, you are not legally obligated to report offenders as of current law as I understand it. But for most of the ministers and counselors likely to read this primer, who do not work out of a more Catholic setting, as it appears to the world, you are seen to have adopted models more in keeping with current secular counseling norms. Much of the ethos we have today as counselors is a blend of the biblical standards of our faith and morals, and the great tools we learn from the psychological camps which are indeed helpful in the care of troubled persons.

I guarantee that you will never encounter more serious circumstances, which will ask you tough questions about where you stand as a pastoral counselor as it concerns a person's right to privacy, than you will ministering to sexually broken people, including homosexuals. There is no area of counseling ministry more challenged by the culture, or that is more vulnerable to lawsuits through both civil and criminal courts, than on the subject of dealing with issues and behaviors stemming from homosexuality. The minister who works in this area in the future will likely be more at risk for jail time, because he either did not report something to the authorities, or because his advice was later resented by the client, who sometime after decided to defame the counselor or minister on some hate-speech accusation. You will also encounter people who want to turn to God, but have violated a law, perhaps having done serious harm to another, and do not want to face prison or public shame. You will have Christians who do not understand why you would work with a person who has done such harm to people they know and love. (When I make recommendations about networking with other ministers and pastors, here is one reason).

So, minister, pastor, counselor, have you thought about the privacy of the counseling experience and where you stand on these issues? Whatever your stance, do you make it very plain to those you counsel where you draw the lines? If you do consider yourself mandated to report extremely serious matters to the officers of the law, then you must, out of Christian integrity, make that very clear early in your counseling relationship with your client/church member. Unfortunately, your approach will probably curtail or negate their ability to reach out for help to find the grace and the forgiveness that they so desperately need. In circumstances where the clients see no avenue of success, when they begin to hate the path they are on but find no place of hope or grace, they will seriously begin the consideration of suicide. In such despair they will often push God out of what is left of their conscience, and give themselves over to the life that has imprisoned them.

Final Comments

Pastors, ministers, and churches:

Be very concerned about professional confidentiality. Keep all personal information under lock and key. Never speak or offer information about your client under any circumstances without proper waivers signed by client and caregiver on both ends of the transfer. Keep current on such laws and practices in the state in which you minister. Take responsibility for your client's privacy.

Pastors, ministers, and churches:

Work together in your local communities to help one another minister to your brothers and sisters who struggle in this area. Work with one another to keep a brother "churched," during a time he may be separated from his own congregation and family while things settle down and heal up. Work together to keep the broken reed from being destroyed.

Pastors, ministers, and churches:

Consider reviewing again the parachurch ministries, institutions, and care centers that do front-line work in this area. Support them and help them survive. There are mainline Christian enterprises like Focus on the Family who provide wonderful educational materials to help us in our local work. There are also organizations like NARTH, and others who do professional and scientific research to aid in our defense in the courts of the land. EXODUS has taken a lot of heat, as they have gathered men and women trying hard to leave the world of homosexuality and have ministered to them and encouraged them. Consider sending some of your own men and women to school, and assist them in graduate-level clinical work, and bring them back to your communities to help in the next generation.

Pastors, ministers, and churches:

Consider as a community of churches in your local area, to support one of the Christian legal defense teams. These are men and women who have become attorneys at law, who are dedicating their lives, and their careers to helping the church survive in this and the next generation. They may be doing the most important work of all. If the churches of our land cannot proclaim the gospel and call people to repentance from sin in order to inherit the kingdom of God, we are all done. This kind of work takes big bucks, and it would be just a few dollars from many contributors if we would organize. I live in a small city, about 100,000 in rural America. But there are 212 churches in my county, and all of them can afford 25 dollars a month.

Pastors, ministers, and churches:

Consider at both the local and state level to begin having an organized Christian voice in the office of your local mayor, your school board, your county, and your state. In the political world, numbers count. Pay attention to the issues and the challenges in your own community, and do not be afraid to speak up for your faith, your church, and your freedom. We have done that more or less successfully in pro-life issues, here is an equally great cause.

Pastors, ministers, and churches:

Does your area have a ministers' meeting, or groupings of churches that are interconnected in some way? What are your conservative churches doing in your local area to challenge those sister congregations which are embracing these serious issues and being absorbed by them? Where are the people in your Christian community who have not bowed the knee to Baal? Since the vows at ordination services are almost entirely to God, not to the churches, what are ministers in your area doing to hold one another accountable for the gospel they are proclaiming, and for their faithfulness to the Word of God?

Pastors, ministers, and churches:

What are you doing among your own people, in your own congregation, to assure the continued orthodoxy of faith? How many kids in your own church families see nothing wrong in the message of the homosexual community and the gay agenda? Here is the challenge question for the day: how often are your pulpits used to offer pastoral sermons that illumine biblical principles and illustrate how to live them on the basic issue of biblical human sexuality? Do your teachings offer a good critique of the ways of the enemy who works to name that which is evil as good, and that which is good as evil? Or as John Stott would frame it, do you preach with the Bible in one hand and with the daily newspaper in the other? How have you taught and modeled to your people the balance of ministering grace and loving sinners struggling as this book describes, while holding on to them as brothers or sisters, and encouraging them in their faithfulness to Christ?

We need each other, we never should have thought otherwise. And while I pray that the visible church will one day be as one as she may be to God invisibly, I am personally proud to assist, and stand with any man or woman of God who will hold on to the broken and bruised and try yet again to encourage them home, doing all we can together to show them the way.

Pastors, ministers, and churches:

There are some homes that have some really dark places in them. Do all you can to make sure your church home is filled with the things people from these homes are truly hungry for instead of the fodder the devil has been feeding them, i.e., the light of the word, the truth of His testimony, the love of Jesus, and the grace and forgiveness of God in the hearts of His people. May your light truly shine to those so wounded by the enemies of Christ.

In the introductory chapter, I started these several essays with a prayer, copied from the 1979 version of the Book of Common Prayer. So, let me finish with this. I pray that there is something in this book that will help you when called upon to minister grace and hope to those who are having a really difficult time in believing that is possible. We as Christians lose too many of our wounded to the Enemy. Let's do what we can to get them back.

May God bless you as you minister the means of grace, and the hope of glory to His people. May God bless your ministry in Christ. Please pray for mine as well.

Annotated Bibliography & Resources

Author's preface: The books and other resource materials listed below are some of the very best in publication. It is a greatly abbreviated list of what is available, but serves to point you to a selection of the most helpful titles we use regularly in ministry. *All* of them are worthy reading, but I have placed an asterisk beside one or more books in several categories that I deem to be a good representative volume on the subject, with exceptionally insightful, helpful content.

Understanding Homosexuality
(Practical helps for struggler and helpers)

*Consiglio, Dr. William. *Homosexual No More: Practical Strategies for Christians Overcoming Homosexuality*. Canada: Victor Books, 1991.

Dailey, Timothy J. *Dark Obsession: The Tragedy and Threat of the Homosexual Lifestyle*. Nashville: Broadman & Holman, 2003.

*Dallas, Joe. *Desires in Conflict*. Eugene, OR: Harvest House, 1991.

_____. *The Game Plan: The Men's 30-Day Strategy for Attaining Sexual Integrity*. Nashville: W Publishing Group, 2005.

*Davies, Bob, and Lori Rentzel. *Coming Out of Homosexuality: New Freedom for Men & Women*. Downers Grove, IL: Inter-Varsity, 1993.

Davies, Bob, with Lela Gibert. *Portraits of Freedom: 14 People Who Came Out of Homosexuality.* Downers Grove, IL: InterVarsity, 2001.

Foster, David Kyle. *Sexual Healing.* Ventura, CA: Regal, 2005.

Haley, Mike. *101 Frequently Asked Questions about Homosexuality.* Eugene, OR: Harvest House, 2004.

*Love Won Out Series. *The Truth Comes Out: The Roots and Causes of Male Homosexuality.* Booklet from Focus on the Family.

Medinger, Alan. *Growth into Manhood.* Colorado Springs: Shaw, 2000.

*Sneeringer, Christine. *The Heart of the Matter: The Roots and Causes of Female Homosexuality.* Love Won Out Series. Booklet from Focus on the Family.

*Worthen, Anita, and Bob Davies. *Someone I Love Is Gay: How Family and Friends Can Respond.* Downers Grove, IL: InterVarsity, 1996.

Same-Gender Issues for Women

*Paulk, Anne. *Restoring Sexual Identity: Hope for Women Who Struggle with Same-Gender Attraction.* Eugene, OR: Harvest House, 2003.

*Sneeringer, Christine. *The Heart of the Matter: The Roots and Causes of Female Homosexuality.* Love Won Out Series. Booklet from Focus on the Family.

Whitehead, Briar. *Craving for Love: Relationship Addiction, Homosexuality and the God Who Heals.* Grand Rapids: Kregel, 2003.

Judeo-Christian Authors Dealing with Homosexuality from a Scientific, Genetic, and Psychological Framework

*Jones, Stanton L., and Mark A. Yarnhouse. *Homosexuality: The Use of Scientific Research in the Church's Moral Debate.* Downers Grove, IL: InterVarsity, 2000.

*Nicolosi, Dr. Joseph. *Reparative Therapy of Male Homosexuality: A New Clinical Approach.* Northvale, NJ: Jason Aronson, 1991.

Reisman, Dr. Judith A., et al. *Kinsey, Sex and Fraud: The Indoctrination of a People.* Lafayette, LA: Huntington House, 1990.

*Satinover, Jeffrey, M.D. *Homosexuality and the Politics of Truth.* Grand Rapids: Baker Books, 1996.

Van Den Aardweg, Gerard J.M. *The Battle for Normality: A Guide for Self-Therapy for Homosexuality.* San Francisco: Ignatius Press, 1997.

Whitehead, Neil and Briar. *My Genes Made Me Do It! A Scientific Look at Sexual Orientation.* Lafayette, LA: Huntington House, 1999.

Authors Specifically Instructing Parents on Prevention of Homosexuality and Identifying Child and Adolescent Sexual Problems

The first two titles below should be on every Christian leader's shelf and in every church library. They are essential reading!

*Dobson, James. *Bringing Up Boys.* Wheaton, IL: Tyndale House, 2001.

*Nicolosi, Joseph and Linda. *A Parent's Guide to Preventing Homosexuality.* Downers Grove, IL: InterVarsity, 2002.

Rekers, Dr. George A. *Handbook of Child and Adolescent Sexual Problems.* New York: Lexington Books, 1995.

Schmierer, Don. *An Ounce of Prevention: Preventing the Homosexual Condition in Today's Youth.* Nashville: Word, 1998.

Authors Dealing with the Bible and Theology Related to Homosexuality

Gagnon, Robert A.J. *The Bible and Homosexual Practice: Texts and Hermeneutics.* Nashville: Abingdon, 2001.

Love Won Out Series. *Responding to Pro-Gay Theology: What Does the Bible Really Say?* Booklet from Focus on the Family.

*Schmidt, Thomas E. *Straight & Narrow*. Downers Grove, IL: InterVarsity, 1995.

Stott, John. *Homosexual Partnerships? Why Same-Sex Relationships Are Not a Christian Option*. Downers Grove, IL: InterVarsity, 1985.

White, James R., and Jeffrey D. Niell. *The Same Sex Controversy: Defending and Clarifying the Bible's Message about Homosexuality*. Minneapolis: Bethany House, 2002.

*Wold, Donald J. *Out of Order: Homosexuality in the Bible and the Ancient Near East*. Grand Rapids: Baker, 1998. *(Unfortunately out of print but available through sources such as Half.com & Amazon used books.)*

Considerations for a Christian Response

*Chambers, Alan, and the Leadership Team at Exodus International. *God's Grace and the Homosexual Next Door*. Eugene, OR: Harvest House, 2006.

Dallas, Joe. *How Should We Respond: An Exhortation to the Church on Loving the Homosexual*. Love Won Out Series. Booklet from Focus on the Family.

_____. *When Homosexuality Hits Home: What to Do When a Loved One Says They're Gay*. Eugene, OR: Harvest House, 2004.

Grenz, Stanley J. *Welcoming but Not Affirming*. Louisville, KY: Westminster John Knox Press, 1998.

Love Won Out Series. *When Someone Says, "I'm Gay."* Booklet from Focus on the Family.

Thompson, Chad W. *Loving Homosexuals as Jesus Would: A Fresh Christian Approach*. Grand Rapids: Brazos Press, 2004.

Authors Dealing with the Gay Agenda and Politics

Bayer, Ronald. *Homosexuality and American Psychiatry: The Politics of Diagnosis*. Princeton, NJ: Princeton University Press, 1987. *(This is a detailed, historical account of the political intrigue and intimidation behind the removal of homosexuality as a mental disorder in the DSM (Diagnostic Statistical Manual of Psychiatric Disorders.)*

*Dallas, Joe. *Straight Answers: Exposing the Myths and Facts about Homosexuality*. Love Won Out Series. Booklet from Focus on the Family.

*_____. *A Strong Delusion: Confronting the "Gay Christian" Movement*. Eugene, OR: Harvest House, 1996.

Dannemeyer, William. *Shadow in the Land: Homosexuality in America*. San Francisco: Ignatius Press, 1989.

Dobson, James. *Marriage under Fire: Why We Must Win This War*. Sisters, OR: Multnomah, 2004.

Grant, George, and Mark A. Horne. *Legislating Immorality: The Homosexual Movement Comes Out of the Closet*. Chicago: Moody Press, 1993.

*Love Won Out Series. *Teaching Captivity? How the Pro-Gay Agenda Is Affecting Our Schools . . . and How You Can Make a Difference*. Booklet from Focus on the Family.

Mazzalongo, Michael, ed. *Gay Rights or Wrongs*. Joplin, MO: College Press, 1995.

*Sears, Alan, and Craig Osten. *The Homosexual Agenda: Exposing the Principle Threat to Religious Freedom Today*. Nashville: Broadman & Holman, 2003.

*Socarides, Charles W., M.D. *Homosexuality: A Freedom Too Far*. Phoenix: Adam Margrave Books, 1995.

Sprigg, Peter. *OUTRAGE: How Gay Activists and Liberal Judges Are Trashing Democracy to Redefine Marriage*. Washington, DC: Regnery, 2004.

Key *Pro-Gay* Authors Dealing with Gay Theology, Activism, and Politics

Besen, Wayne R. *Anything but Straight: Unmasking the Scandals and Lies behind the Ex-Gay Myth*. New York: Harrington Park Press, 2003.

Boswell, John. *Christianity, Social Tolerance and Homosexuality.* Chicago: The University of Chicago Press, 1980. *(This book is quoted more frequently in pro-gay "Christian" literature than any other single volume.)*

Goss, Robert. *Jesus Acted Up: A Gay and Lesbian Manifesto.* San Francisco: HarperCollins, 1993. *(This book lays out a theological and philosophical construct for overthrowing traditional, orthodox Christianity and marriage. It is a guide for revolutionaries—utterly sobering.)*

McNeil, John J. *The Church and the Homosexual.* 4th printing. Boston: Beacon Press, 1993. *(A well-known homosexual, Episcopal priest, and gay activist, McNeil's gay theology has found tremendous acceptance in liberal denominations and churches.)*

Stevenson, Michael R., and Jeanine C. Cogan, eds. *Everyday Activism: A Handbook for Lesbian, Gay, and Bisexial People and Their Allies.* New York: Routledge, 2003.

White, Mel. *Stranger at the Gate: To Be Gay and Christian in America.* New York: Plume Books, 1995.

Author's note: *I first met Mel's parents who were students in the Biblical Counseling School of the Pacific & Asia Christian University (YWAM—Youth With A Mission) in Kona, Hawaii, in 1981. I was a guest lecturer teaching a week-long seminar on homosexuality. In 1984, my young family relocated to Santa Cruz, California, where I attended college. We lived just blocks from the Whites in Scotts Valley, California. They were missionaries at the time. This is their son Mel's story of growing up with same-gender issues in a conservative Christian family and Church. It is worth the read if only to better understand the agony, confusion, and psyche of Christians struggling with homosexuality. It provides insight into the internal conflict that often propels people to reach faulty conclusions and embrace the Lie out of the attrition and desperation they experience.*

Authors Dealing with Sexual Addiction

Arterburn, Stephen, and Fred Stoeker. *Every Man's Battle.* Colorado Springs: Waterbrook Press, 2000. *(There's also a workbook with this and another title dedicated to teen boys.)*

Carnes, Patrick. *Out of the Shadows: Understanding Sexual Addiction*. Minneapolis: CompCare, 1983.

*Carnes, Patrick, David Delmonico, and Elizabeth Griffin. *In the Shadows of the Net: Breaking Free of Compulsive Online Sexual Behavior*. Center City, MN: Hazelden, 2001.

Laaser, Dr. Mark R. *Healing the Wounds of Sexual Addiction*. Grand Rapids: Zondervan, 2004.

_____. *A L.I.F.E. Guide: A Workbook for Living in Freedom Every Day in Sexual Wholeness and Integrity*. Fairfax: Xulon Press, 2003.

*_____. *The Pornography Trap: Setting Pastors and Laypersons Free from Addiction*. Kansas City: Beacon Hill, 2002.

*Schaumburg, Harry W. *False Intimacy: Understanding the Struggle of Sexual Addiction*. Colorado Springs: NavPress, 1997.

Weiss, Robert. *Cruise Control: Understanding Sex Addiction in Gay Men*. Los Angeles: Alyson Books, 2005.

White, John. *Eros Redeemed: Breaking the Stranglehold of Sexual Sin*. Downers Grove, IL: InterVarsity, 1993.

Willingham, Russell. *Breaking Free: Understanding Sexual Addiction and the Healing Power of Jesus*. Downers Grove, IL: InterVarsity, 1999.

Related Issues for Men

Ensley, Mike. *Emotional Dependency for Guys*. Orlando, FL: Exodus International, 2007.

Hart, Archibald D. *The Sexual Man: Masculinity without Guilt*. Dallas: Word, 1994.

*McGee, Robert. *Father Hunger*. Ann Arbor, MI: Servant Publications, 1993.

*Osterhaus, James. *Bonds of Iron: Forging Lasting Male Relationships*. Chicago: Moody Press, 1994.

Payne, Leanne. *Crisis in Masculinity*. Grand Rapids: Baker Books, 1995.

Pittman, Frank, M.D. *Man Enough: Fathers, Sons, and the Search for Masculinity.* New York: Berkley, 1993.

Sexual Abuse

> **Author's note:** There are, of course, many excellent books that have been published on this subject by professional psychologists. They provide invaluable research and insights into both the impact of sexual abuse, and therapeutic work with individuals and families in recovery. I utilize them as reference material in my own pastoral counseling frequently. However, many of these books contain material that also recognizes and affirms homosexuality as a *normal* identity and lifestyle choice—which I absolutely disagree with. Therefore, for the purposes of this book, I will only be including books written by authors who uphold Christian orthodoxy in sexual matters (so far as I am aware).

*Allender, Dr. Dan B. *The Wounded Heart: Hope for Adult Victims of Childhood Sexual Abuse.* Colorado Springs: Navpress, 2008.

*_____. *The Wounded Heart Workbook: A Companion Workbook.* Colorado Springs: Navpress, 2008.

Frank, Jan. *Door of Hope: Recognizing and Resolving the Pains of Your Past.* Nashville: Thomas Nelson, 1995.

Heitritter, Lynn, and Jeanette Vought. *Helping Victims of Sexual Abuse: A Sensitive Biblical Guide for Counselors, Victims, and Families.* Grand Rapids: Bethany House, 2006.

Langberg, Diane Mandt. *On the Threshold of Hope.* Carol Stream, IL: Tyndale House, 1999.

Emotional Incest, Codependency, and Boundary Issues

*Adams, Kenneth M. *Silently Seduced: When Parents Make Their Children Partners—Understanding Covert Incest.* Deerfield Beach, FL: Health Communications, 1991.

Cloud, Henry, and John Townsend. *Boundaries.* Grand Rapids: Zondervan, 1992.

Groom, Nancy. *From Bondage to Bonding: Escaping Codependency, Embracing Biblical Love*. Colorado Springs: NavPress, 1991.

*Love, Dr. Patricia. *The Emotional Incest Syndrome: What to Do When a Parent's Love Rules Your Life*. New York: Bantam Books, 1990.

*Rentzel, Lori. *Emotional Dependency*. Downers Grove, IL: Inter-Varsity, 1990.

Genogram and Family Systems Assessment

Genogram *resources can be very helpful in your assessment of an individual as seen within the wrapping of their family-of-origin. They are particularly useful for plotting cross-generational family pathology, and can add a dimension to family systems analysis. There are occasions where the use of a genogram can help lift a great deal of personal shame off of the individual client who is struggling with deep emotional pain. For software programs and other related resources, contact:* **www. genogram.org**—GenoWare, Inc., 1826 Crestvale Place NE, Atlanta, GA 30345, FAX: 866-477-8305. **GenoWare@genogram.org**.

DeMaria, Rita, Gerald Weeks, and Larry Hof. *FOCUSED GENO-GRAMS: Intergenerational Assessment of Individuals, Couples, and Families*. New York: Brunner-Routledge, 1999.

McGoldrick, Monica, Randy Gerson, and Sueli Petry. *GENOGRAMS: Assessment and Intervention*, 3rd ed. New York: W.W. Norton, 2008.

Family System Concepts *provide a wealth of insights into the interpersonal dynamics of a "stuck" system. From one's own family of origin to the local church, each operates as a "family system." Below is a short list of my favorites. A solid understanding of the Bowen theory and the use of genograms are critical tools in ministering pastoral care to the sexually broken.*

Bowen, Murray, and Michael E. Kerr. *Family Evaluation*. Ontario: Penguin Books Canada, 1988.

Friedman, Edwin H. *Generation to Generation: Family Process in Church and Synagogue*. New York: Guilford Press, 1985.

(This book is a must for Christian leaders. Written in an anecdotal format, it is especially helpful in illustrating ways to effect change within "stuck" family systems. One will have a deepened understanding of Bowen's concept of equilibrium, and how one person can often change the dynamic of a whole group, sometimes with the most passive changes to the system. This is a very helpful tool for pastors dealing with congregational families.)

Gilbert, Roberta M. *The Eight Concepts of Bowen Theory.* Basye and Falls Church, VA: Leading Systems Press, 2004.

Kerr, Michael E., and Murray Bowen. *Family Evaluation.* New York: W.W. Norton, 1988.

Christian Leaders, the Law, and Ethics

Author's note: Christian leaders who regularly minister to very broken people dealing with sexual issues, must keep themselves current on their own state's laws. This is an ongoing necessity, especially in this heightened social climate of accusing Christians with hate crimes, when they are simply teaching biblical truth and upholding the right of the person seeking help to choose their own life course, by seeking reparative therapy and/or spiritual guidance and mentoring from whom they so choose.

You need to carefully observe appropriate boundaries in your work with others. It can come back to bite you in unexpected ways. Establish safeguards for your sake and the sake of others, and make sure you have one or more persons to whom you are accountable in your life, by your own wise choice. One of the best books I have read on the matter of sexual misconduct is listed below. It is a worthy read, perhaps a powerful, wise preventative investment on your part.

*Hammar, Richard R. *Pastor, Church & Law.* 3rd ed. Mathews, NC: Christian Ministry Resources, 2000.

*Mosgofian, Peter, and George Ohlschlager. *Sexual Misconduct in Counseling Ministry.* Dallas: Word, 1995.

Ohlschlager, George, and Peter Mosgofian. *Law for the Christian Counselor: A Guidebook for Clinicians and Pastors.* Dallas: Word, 1992.

Trull, Joe E., and James E. Carter. *Ministerial Ethics: Moral Formation for Church Leaders.* Grand Rapids: Baker Academic, 2004.

The Alliance Defense Fund is a legal alliance defending the right to hear and speak the Truth through strategy, training, funding, and litigation. (Description copied from ADF.) Contact at: **www.alliancedefensefund.org/main/default.aspx**, or at Alliance Defense Fund, 15100 N. 90th St., Scottsdale, AZ 85260 (1-800-835-5233).

Family Research Council (FRC) was founded in 1983 as an organization dedicated to the promotion of marriage and family and the sanctity of human life in national policy. Through books, pamphlets, media appearances, public events, debates, and testimony, FRC's team of experienced policy experts review data and analyze proposals that impact family law and policy in Congress and the executive branch. FRC also strives to assure that the unique attributes of the family are recognized and respected through the decisions of the courts and regulatory bodies. (Description copied from the FRC website.) **www.frc.org/**

Internet Resources

Author's preface: There are three superb organizations that continue to play a pivotal role in providing resources, educating the Church at large, and actively countering the pro-gay agenda in our society. Every pastor and church should be familiar with these organizations and their resources. All of these sites provide bookstores with tremendous materials.

1) Exodus International: www.exodus-international.org/

Exodus is a nonprofit, interdenominational Christian organization promoting the message of *Freedom from homosexuality through the power of Jesus Christ.* Since 1976, Exodus has grown to include over 120 local ministries in the USA and Canada. We are also linked with other Exodus world regions outside of North America, totaling over 150 ministries in 17 countries. Within both the Christian and secular communities Exodus has challenged those who respond to homosexuals with ignorance and fear, and those who uphold homosexuality as a valid orientation. These extremes fail to convey the fullness of redemption found in Jesus Christ, a gift that is available to all who commit their life and their sexuality to him.

Exodus is the largest Christian referral and information network dealing with homosexual issues in the world. A list of current qualified member ministries is available on their website (see *Find A Ministry*). Each listing is an independent organization, which has met Exodus's criteria for membership. Most of our members are "lay" (nonprofessional) ministries, while some are professional counseling centers and some are churches' ministries. Each provides unique services and resources. Our member ministries provide support for individuals who want to recover from homosexuality, as well as provide support for their family (parents, spouses, children, relatives) and friends.

The EXODUS website offers a wealth of information including a large library of excellent articles, testimonies, bookstore, and an outreach program for teens and college age youth. EXODUS holds an annual conference. Each year, over 1,000 men, women, youth, pastors, therapists, spouses, parents, and other interested persons come together for a unique gathering of instruction and celebration. Besides powerful worship and inspirational messages, dozens of workshops are presented on counseling, relationships, sexual struggles, societal issues, support for family and friends, ministry development, and various other topics. This five-day event is held annually in late July, in different cities throughout North America. (Description copied from Exodus website.)

2) NARTH (The National Association for Research and Therapy of Homosexuality), 16633 Ventura Blvd., Suite 1340, Encino, CA 91436-1801. Phone: 1-818-789-4440 or 1-888-364-4744. Joseph Nicolosi, Ph.D. Fax: 805-373-5084. Internet address: **www.narth.com**.

NARTH is a non-profit, educational organization dedicated to affirming a complementary, male-female model of gender and sexuality. Founded in 1992, we are a community of psychiatrists, psychologists, certified social workers, professional and pastoral counselors and other behavioral scientists, as well as laymen from a wide variety of backgrounds such as law, religion, and education. We welcome the participation of all individuals who will join us in the pursuit of these goals. (Description copied from NARTH website).

3) FOCUS ON THE FAMILY: www.focusonthefamily.com. 1-800-232-6459

Dr. James Dobson and the Focus on the Family organization have been in the vanguard, helping educate the Church how to understand and minister to persons struggling with same-gender confusion. A family-oriented ministry, that remains relevant in an ever-changing culture and intentional in our efforts to reach out to today's family.

4) LOVE WON OUT (FOCUS ON THE FAMILY) www.lovewonout.com

The primary event is a dynamic one-day conference which, through more than 20 different sessions, addresses the many and varied issues related to homosexuality from a Christian perspective. Nationally known experts tackle everything from why some people struggle with same-sex attraction to the profound significance of God's created intent for sexuality. Parents, family members, and friends learn how to reach out with the gospel to loved ones who are living homosexually. Pastors, counselors, and educators are equipped to articulate the Christian worldview on sexuality within their spheres of influence. And those who are on their own journey toward overcoming unwanted same-sex attraction hear inspiring stories of men and women radically transformed by God's forgiving and transforming love. (Description copied from LOVE WON OUT website.)

Additional organizations:

P-Fox (Parents and Friends of Ex-Gays) www.P-Fox.org

PFOX is not a therapeutic or counseling organization. PFOX supports families, advocates for the ex-gay community, and educates the public on sexual orientation. Each year thousands of men, women, and teens with unwanted same-sex attractions make the personal decision to leave homosexuality. However, there are those who refuse to respect that decision. Consequently, formerly gay persons are reviled simply because they dare to exist! Without PFOX, ex-gays would have no voice in a hostile environment. PFOX families unconditionally love their children. PFOX parents recognize our children for the wonderful young men and women they are. PFOX families do not label children based on who they are attracted to—feelings can and do change. PFOX families allow for differences of opinion: we do not place requirements on our children nor do they place them on us. That's what unconditional love means—loving each other even when we do not agree.

PFOX contact information: PO Box 561, Ft. Belvoir, VA 22060. Phone: 703-739-8220. Regina Griggs. Email: **griggs@erols. com** (for information on local chapters). Internet: **www.p-fox. com**. (Description copied from PFOX website.)

On Making Professional Counseling Referrals

Author's preface: *After thirty years of ministry in this specialized counseling field, I wish I could say that all Christian counselors are equipped to effectively work with people struggling with homosexuality; I cannot. Quite honestly, most do not have adequate insight, understanding, or the training to work with* **SGS** *(same-gender strugglers). I have had to undo considerable damage done by "professional" Christian counselors. Here is my strong recommendation:*

1) Contact **EXODUS** (via their website or by phone) to locate the nearest affiliate ministry. You must understand that there are significant differences between these ministries. Individual referral agencies are affiliated with diverse faith backgrounds and denominations. The various ministries provide widely different services and *ministry* approaches (e.g., professional counseling, lay counseling, no counseling, support groups or not, etc.). Only a small percentage of EXODUS ministries have professionally trained, licensed counselors on staff. You will need to help determine whether a specific local ministry is capable of effectively addressing the unique needs of a given situation with the level of professional services you are seeking.

2) If there is no ministry within a reasonable driving distance of where you are located, some counselors will arrange phone

counseling on a fee scale. If you are fortunate enough to have one or more known and trusted Christian counselors in your area, you should explore their experience and success working with people struggling with SGA. Even though it may not be a specialty area for them, they may know enough to be of help—at least initially.

3) If you are in the Midwest, you can contact our ministry: **Kent Paris, MA, Director, Nehemiah Ministries, P.O. Box 773, Urbana, IL 61803. Office: 1-217-344-4636. www.nehemiah online.com**

4) **NARTH (1-888-364-4744, www.narth.com)**. While NARTH is not an expressly Christian-based organization, they are unmatched in their effectiveness working within the professional psychological community when it comes to homosexuality. They are networked with members (psychiatrists, psychologists, medical doctors, and therapists) throughout the U.S. working within a psychoanalytic tradition to assist those seeking change. I would especially encourage pastors and Christian counselors to seriously consider a NARTH referral in circumstances where a person is experiencing trans-gender confusion (a male or female thinking they are or wishing they were actually the opposite gender. These cases are normally exceedingly complex, and you will want the best and most professional referral resource at hand. NARTH is unmatched in countering the unproven theory that homosexuality is inborn, and that people born *gay* cannot change. Their website is a treasure trove of invaluable research information.

5) **FOCUS ON THE FAMILY**. Besides pointing you in the direction of EXODUS, they may be aware of professional Christian counselors in your area that you are unaware of.

6) **Rapha Christian Counseling.** Phone: 800-383-4673. Rapha has branches in several cities, offering counseling for a variety of problems including various sexual disorders and sexual addiction issues.

7) **Minirth-Meier New Life Treatment Center.** 2100 N Collins Rd, Richardson, TX 75080. Phone: 214-669-1733. Fax: 800-778-5855. **Minirth-Meier** also has branches throughout the U.S.

Resources Regarding Pornography
(including Internet Filter Programs)

(All descriptions copied directly from product websites.)

Porn Free Youth. P.O. Box 131, Cortland, OH 44410. Matt DeBenedictis. Phone: 330-638-1988. **www.standtrue.com/porn freeyouth**. A youth-based organization that educates people on the harms of pornography and all other sexual issues while helping those who are striving to be pure.

Safe Eyes™ has earned *PC Magazine's* Editor's Choice for parental-control software two years running! Filter objectionable material—including social networking, IM, email, and websites—while receiving immediate alerts if questionable activity occurs! You get it all—weekly reports, PC and Mac compatibility, usage on up to three computers—for one low price!

Bsafe Online™ is an award-winning filtering and online security solution protecting both your family and your PC for one low cost. **Bsafe Online** puts parents in control of when the Internet can be accessed and what websites are visited, records and monitors IM conversations, and sends a weekly report of all Internet activity.

Covenant Eyes™ Accountability offers several software programs designed to help a user learn to surf the Internet with integrity, by personal choice. The accountability entails one or more persons the user selects who will receive a weekly, full, detailed list of every site visited. **www.covenanteyes.com/**

pkFamily™ (PROMISE KEEPERS™) has partnered with **Digital Systems Support**, Inc. to offer the most advanced filtering technology available to date! With years of experience in implementing filtering technology on a national basis, Digital Systems Support, Inc. is recognized as the pioneer and leader in the filtered Internet Service Provider industry. Digital Systems Support, Inc. employs patented filtering technology that has consistently rated superior to the competition based on independent studies, tests, and evaluations. You can read more at: **www.pkfamily.com/filtering.htm**.